Praise for the first edition of *Create Distinction*
(published with the title *Collapse of Distinction*)

"*Collapse of Distinction* is further evidence that Scott McKain is the premiere business communicator of our time.

"Not only has Scott produced extraordinary results in his own businesses by adhering to these principles, but he makes it simple for you to do so as well. By following the easily applied concepts from *Collapse of Distinction*, you will set the standard of excellence for your industry and make your competition irrelevant."

> —JOSEPH MICHELLI, PhD, speaker, consultant, and author of
> *The Starbucks Experience* and *The New Gold Standard: 5 Leadership Principles for Creating a Legendary Customer Experience Courtesy of the Ritz-Carlton Hotel Company*

"Differentiation is not an option in business. In a world where the word 'commodity' has become the norm, Scott McKain clarifies the all-important (and all-profitable) strategy to become *different*, become *distinct*, and become *dominant* in your marketplace. Buy this book. Read it. And put it into practice."

> —JEFFREY GITOMER, author of *The Little Red Book of Selling*

"Scott McKain's latest book, *Collapse of Distinction*, is a *must-read* for any professional or organization attempting to creatively differentiate from the competition."

> —DON HUTSON, co-author of the #1 *New York Times* bestseller
> *The One Minute Entrepreneur*, and CEO of U.S. Learning

"Scott McKain's *Collapse of Distinction* may just save our sanity and common sense with his positive approach to business and life itself."

> —JOE BONSALL, thirty-five-year member of the legendary music group the Oak Ridge Boys and author of the best-selling book *G.I. Joe and Lillie*

"With superb style, storytelling, and rationale, *Collapse of Distinction* is a distinctive piece of business and personal literature."

—Ty Boyd, founder and chairman, Executive Learning Systems

"If I can't tell the difference between you and your competitor, why should I spend my money with you? Scott McKain's new book teaches how to answer that question—the *right* way!"

—Larry Winget, television personality and *New York Times* best-selling author of *People Are Idiots and I Can Prove It*

"*Collapse of Distinction* isn't just a business success book, this is a business *survival* book for the reality of today's marketplace. If customers don't see what makes you different, then you're just a commodity—forced to live or die on price alone. Lucky for us, McKain shows the way to differentiation through strategies that create distinction—generating true separation from your competition."

—Joe Calloway, best-selling author of *A Category of One* and member of the Professional Speakers Hall of Fame

"We no longer have the choice to stay the same. Our world demands that we generate new solutions . . . now! Scott McKain shows us how to grow our way out of this challenging economy. Read this book NOW—you cannot afford to wait any longer."

—Jim Cathcart, author of *Relationship Selling* and recipient of Toastmaster International's "Golden Gavel" award

"Learn how to differentiate in a way that allows you to not only survive, but thrive, in uncertain times. Don't just buy this book; *devour* it, and use it to invent your future now!"

—Terry Paulson, PhD, consultant on change, and author of *Leadership Truths: One Story at a Time*

"The good news about *Collapse of Distinction*? It doesn't call for big dollars—only big thinking. CEOs of organizations large and small can get excited about his plan for real distinction in the marketplace. This book is bound to put passion back in your people, projects, and customers."

—Dianna Booher, author of *The Voice of Authority:*
   10 Communication Strategies Every Leader Needs to Know

"*Collapse of Distinction* clearly shows you practical, powerful, profitable steps to create a competitive advantage so you can out-market, out-sell, and out-service your competition."

—Dr. Tony Alessandra, author of *Collaborative Selling*
   and *The NEW Art of Managing People*

"*Collapse of Distinction* is another masterpiece from the brilliant business mind of Scott McKain. The lessons we learn from his unique perspective can be adapted to any business of any size."

—Patricia Fripp, CSP, CPAE; former president of the National
   Speakers Association

"For thirty-one years as an NFL referee, every time I walked off the field I asked myself if I had left the game better today than I had found it. My intention was to discover ways I could distinguish my performance—not only from others, but also from my previous efforts. *Collapse of Distinction* by Scott McKain tells what it takes to be the best you can be, whether you are running a business or refereeing a Super Bowl. I have never read a book that explains it so well. This is a must read!"

—Dr. Jim Tunney, "Dean of NFL Officials," referee of three Super
   Bowls, member of NFL Hall of Fame, educator, and author of *It's
   the Will, Not the Skill*

CREATE
DISTINCTION

SCOTT MCKAIN

CREATE

DISTINCTION

{ WHAT *to* DO WHEN "GREAT" ISN'T
GOOD ENOUGH *to* GROW YOUR BUSINESS }

GREENLEAF
BOOK GROUP LLC

Published by Greenleaf Book Group Press
Austin, Texas
www.gbgpress.com

First published by Thomas Nelson in 2009 as *Collapse of Distinction*.

Distributed by Greenleaf Book Group LLC

For ordering information or special discounts for bulk purchases, please contact Greenleaf Book Group LLC at PO Box 91869, Austin, TX 78709, 512.891.6100.

Design and composition by Greenleaf Book Group LLC
Cover design by Greenleaf Book Group LLC

Publisher's Cataloging-In-Publication Data
(Prepared by The Donohue Group, Inc.)

McKain, Scott.
  [Collapse of distinction. 2012]
  Create distinction : what to do when "great" isn't good enough to grow your business / Scott McKain.—2nd ed.

    p. ; cm.

  First published as: The collapse of distinction : stand out and move up while your competition fails. Nashville, Tenn. : Thomas Nelson, c2009.
  Includes bibliographical references.
  ISBN: 978-1-60832-426-2

  1. Marketing. 2. Marketing—Management. 3. Success in business. I. Title. II. Title: Collapse of distinction.

HF5415.13 .M37 2013
658.8   2012945723

Part of the Tree Neutral® program, which offsets the number of trees consumed in the production and printing of this book by taking proactive steps, such as planting trees in direct proportion to the number of trees used: www.treeneutral.com

TreeNeutral®

Printed in the United States of America on acid-free paper

12 13 14 15 16 17 10 9 8 7 6 5 4 3 2 1

Second Edition

I am grateful to so many people for so much . . . therefore, it was extraordinarily difficult to select just one person to whom I should dedicate this book.

Until—with the blinding flash of the obvious—I realized that without the inspiration, insight, and involvement of my father, absolutely none of what I appreciate so much about my life would have been possible.

For my dad . . . Dallas M. McKain (June 9, 1929–August 1, 2004)

Continue to Create Distinction

Our goal is to serve as a resource for you in creating the kind of compelling distinction that will continually enhance the results of your business.

We have created a special website to give you the opportunity to obtain the most recent, cutting-edge information, download seminars and podcasts, and share your success stories as you build distinction for your career and your organization.

Simply direct your Internet browser to http://createdistinction.com.

CONTENTS

PREFACE

What happens when you have moved yourself and your organization from "good to great"—only to discover that in today's business world great is no longer good enough for customers and employees?

How can your customers and prospects tell the difference between you and your competition?

What do you need to do to stand out and move up in order to give yourself competitive space in the marketplace?

These were three of the critical questions that I started asking—and that, in my business as a speaker, consultant, and training company owner, I was being asked by my clients—that led to the research and writing of the book you're now reading.

When the original version of this book—then titled *Collapse of Distinction*—was written in 2008 and published in 2009, we were in a period of global economic collapse. The initial manuscript was created, in part, to assist professionals and organizations to survive a horrific financial downturn.

However, since that time, we have fortunately started to recover to some degree—not only from a financial perspective, but from an attitudinal one as well. It seems we have developed the outlook that we are, individually and collectively, going to do whatever it takes to succeed—and not just survive, but thrive—regardless of the immediate economic circumstances.

For this reason, this book has been retitled *Create Distinction: What to Do When "Great" Isn't Good Enough to Grow Your Business* to more accurately reflect the changes in both the market and in our mind-set.

In addition, the opportunity to relaunch this work has presented me the opportunity to update and refine the examples, as well as include the latest thinking on the subject of creating distinction, based on my great experiences presenting this material to hundreds of business audiences around the world and on my exposure to other thinkers and authors on this important topic.

(The examples of my parents' grocery store, the hometown diner, and the extraordinary Taxi Terry remain. If you aren't familiar with them, you soon will be. It seems as though everyone who reads the book comments on these particular stories.)

Finally, this new version also gives us the chance to celebrate the wonderful reviews of the first edition—it was named as one of the top ten business books of the year by several major newspapers—and, most important, to try even harder to make the content both valuable and applicable for you.

Be distinct!

Scott McKain

August 1, 2012

INTRODUCTION

You have probably seen my hometown.

Like legendary Rock and Roll Hall of Fame member John Mellencamp, I was "born in a small town." In fact, my origins were in the same rural town of which he sings.

While we both claim Seymour, Indiana, as our birthplace, I grew up and went to school just a few miles farther south in the even smaller Crothersville, Indiana; both communities were featured in the rock star's classic music videos. I love going back to my hometown, where my mother and my sister still live, as did my grandmother until her recent passing at ninety-eight years of age.

An Illuminating Conversation

An old-timer in my community recently made an interesting observation. "Scott," he said as we reminisced, "it used to be that there were two restaurants here in Crothersville. Not only did the food taste different at Ted's Restaurant than it did at Kern's Grill, but they just plain *felt* different. Each was a reflection of the owner's personality."

I nodded in agreement. Ted's was the spot where we always went after a ball game, took a date for a burger and fries, or simply hung out. Kern's Grill was the place where the men of the community gathered for breakfast each morning back in the late 1960s and 1970s.

During lunch break at school, I sprinted to Kern's so I could join either Mom or Dad for a quick meal. (But never both of them at the same time. We owned the grocery store across the street, and one of my parents always had to stay to run our family business.)

For Ted Zollman, his restaurant was his stage, and we customers were his audience. His smile was as bright as his apron. His flashing blue eyes and natural charisma were as much a part of eating there as the cheeseburgers.

On the other hand, Ted's local competitor, Alvie Kern, would sit in a booth or gruffly stand like a statue behind the counter, often with arms tightly crossed, seldom engaging in ongoing conversation. He was an observer, while his wife and daughter took care of the tables and customers. Kern's Grill was efficient, a great place to grab a meal and go. Before you could exit the door, the white sack in which they had placed your order would display small, and growing, circles of grease. (It was a simpler time before we all knew our HDL and LDL numbers.)

Ted's Restaurant, however, was where you would order a cherry Coke, sit down, and relax, either because a friend was with you or because you knew that sooner or later, one was bound to come in and stay a while.

My old-timer friend continued, "Anymore, our fast food is the same as the fast food up the road. The McDonald's in Seymour is the same as the McDonald's in Scottsburg. In fact, they're all the same from Portland, Oregon, to Portland, Maine. I guess consistency is a good thing, but haven't we reached the point where we've gone overboard?

"The Walmart where we shop is the same as everywhere else . . . and that's pretty much the same as K-Mart and Target. And they all sell the same items anyway. How many places do you *really* need to be able to go buy your Tide detergent?"

He was on a roll: "My insurance agent sells the same stuff as yours, no matter what companies they work for. One has some screaming duck to represent it—another some caveman or lizard. I'm 'in good hands' one place, another is 'on my side,' while another is 'like a good neighbor.' But the problem is, I can't tell one from the next. I know the difference on my street between one of my neighbors and another. So how do I know why one *company* is a better neighbor or 'on my side' more than the other?"

These are great questions.

If you have any professional responsibilities whatsoever—as the CEO of a Fortune 500 company to a small business entrepreneur, as someone at the home office sprinting up the corporate ladder to a salesperson slogging it out in the trenches—this question should keep you tossing and turning at night: how can your customers distinguish you from your competition?

> *Can your customers tell the difference between you and your competition?*

The criterion this senior citizen used to make his determination should terrify you. It should frighten all of us who are trying to grow our businesses and our careers.

"It's just price, I guess!" he deduced. "I sure don't notice any difference between them with service. And I don't know enough about insurance, for example, to really understand the differences between their products. These days, every tree in the forest seems to be exactly alike. It's not just bland," he said. "It's all become the same!"

A Cultural Phenomenon of Epic Proportions

This wise older gentleman was not merely sharing insights regarding his perceptions about the nature of retailing. I believe he was attempting to describe what is becoming a cultural phenomenon as well as a corporate and professional nightmare: the collapse of distinction.

Before we can *create distinction* for ourselves and our organizations in a highly competitive market, we must first examine and understand what has taken place.

There was a time not too long ago when Chevy owners felt superior to those poor souls driving Fords and vice versa. People gained identification through the goods they purchased, the stores where they shopped, the institutions where they invested—no matter the level of price or sophistication of the product. But that is changing.

Over the past several years, we have seen the homogenization of practically everything. The car that I drive probably looks a lot like yours, no matter the nameplate. The big store where I shop almost certainly appears and feels a lot like yours, no matter the logo on the door, no matter the community where it's located. It looks, acts, feels the same—and this is causing a customer revolt.

In a front-page article, the *Wall Street Journal* proclaimed, "The Walmart era . . . is drawing to a close." In other words, we are at the initial stages where the "faster . . . cheaper . . . perfect" generation of customers is now looking for something else from businesses—something profoundly more difficult to deliver. People are craving, even coveting, distinction. [1]

Being different, standing out, getting noticed in a sea of sameness is vital to an organization's sustained growth and profitability. Authors John A. Pearce and Richard B. Robinson agreed in their highly regarded book, *Strategic Management*, saying businesses that stand out "provide a service of *perceived higher value* to buyers."[2]

A Principle of Expanding Importance

At all times, and especially when customers consider times to be tight, they naturally want to spend their money where they receive the highest degree of value. Now is the time to stand out. And when you do, when you highlight your business and yourself, you will find that even a volatile economy is tailor-made for grabbing market share from your competitors.

It would be difficult to find any professional leader, from CEO to sales consultant, who would vote against standing out and looking better than the competition. Everyone is in favor of it, yet few know how to go about making distinction into reality.

The fact is few organizations really *change*; instead, they merely *shuffle*. They reorganize, add managers, subtract staff, outsource, relocate offices, put more people in the field, enhance support from the corporate headquarters—all in the hope of engineering advantages they trust will distance themselves from their competition. Such activities, however, rarely create the elements necessary to inspire distinction.

By understanding the collapse of distinction and implementing strategies to highlight yourself and your organization, you can create greater space between you and your competition.

A Passion for Distinction

If you approach today's marketplace with a tepid, modest, and moderate approach to gaining distinction in your field of endeavor, you had better start getting ready. Unless you become vibrant and committed to making your efforts distinct, your customers will move on.

If you cannot find it within yourself to become emotional, committed, engaged, and, yes, fervent about differentiation, then you had better be prepared to take your place among that vast throng of the mediocre who are judged by their customers solely on the basis of price. It is the singularly worst place to be in all of business.

If you aren't willing to create distinction for yourself in your profession—and for your organization in the marketplace—then prepare to take your seat in the back, with the substantial swarm of the similar, where tedium reigns supreme.

If this seems a bit dramatic, just drive down the main street of most rural or suburban towns and see the deserted storefronts that once housed businesses of all types. They now sit silently as poignant monuments to the organizations that have become casualties of the collapse of distinction.

But don't worry.

You hold in your hands a simple, practical road map to understand why, seemingly all of a sudden, everything seems so much the same. In addition, this book should serve as a guide to assist you in creating the distinction required to make your organization stand apart from the competitors in your industry.

To craft this information, I consulted with and lectured to some of the world's most dynamic organizations. I've created successful businesses myself, and have had a long and diverse career as a speaker, consultant, and author. However, my primary goal here is not to promote my businesses but to be the catalyst that causes you to think—and think deeply—about yours.

What's in Store for You?

You already know you have to stand out to get noticed. My job is to help you do just that. To accomplish our mutual mission, I'll present some background into how this collapse of distinction came about in the marketplace, because no great changes ever happen without some degree of historical perspective.

Then I'll offer a brief illustration of what has been the typical approach of most organizations, regardless of their size or products. (These traditional steps have, for the most part, failed miserably.)

Finally, I'll give you several basic yet specific ideas regarding how you can develop tactics that will make you and your organization distinct.

Meeting the baseline expectations of your customers is not enough. Therefore, I will provide for you, at the conclusion of this journey toward distinction, several additional resources that are immediately available and constantly updated. I hope *Create Distinction* will make a valuable contribution to your organization and your career, as well as provide an experience of the very attribute we are examining.

Executive Summary

At the conclusion of each chapter, you'll find a short executive summary of the major points of that chapter. The goal of the review is to give you not just a quick, one-paragraph rehash, but instead to lay out a more intensive compendium that provides the format for you to return and review the material with a quick skim.

In addition—and many readers of the first edition found this to be one of the greatest values of the book—this summary can produce your "talking points" as you describe the material and discuss the points with your colleagues. The outline below summarizes the main points of the introduction you've just read.

I.   Everything seems the same.

    A. The points of differentiation between businesses across the nation have been practically eliminated.

    B. This phenomenon makes it much more difficult for your customers to distinguish a difference between you and your competitors.

II. This challenge is expanding in significance.

    A. The main street of almost any midsize town includes closed storefronts of businesses that failed to distinguish themselves.

    B. If your customers cannot differentiate you in some other way, then they will fall back upon the one point where they can always discover a distinction—price.

    C. Price is the single worst point of differentiation for any organization in any industry.

    D. Lower prices lead to lower margins, which, in turn, lead to fewer resources for developing our people and enhancing our products.

III. Distinction requires passion.

    A. Most organizations do not change. They merely shuffle.

1. They reorganize, add, or change management, subtract staff, outsource, relocate, and more—all in the hope of stumbling onto something that will reconnect them with customers.

2. Few of these efforts create the elements necessary to inspire distinction.

B. If you cannot create distinction for your business—and differentiation from your competition—you are doomed to mediocrity in today's changing and highly challenging market.

IV. The main objectives of *Create Distinction* are to:

A. Provide a road map for understanding how this phenomenon of "sameness" happened—and what you can do about it.

B. Be a guide to assist you in making your business—and yourself—distinct in the marketplace.

C. Outline strategies for making a difference that will endear you to customers—and make you enduring as an organization and a professional.

Action Steps, Questions, and Ideas

At the end of each chapter there are a few questions for you to consider and some action steps for you to plan as you complete your journal or notebook and prepare to attack the collapse of distinction. Start by thinking and making notes as suggested below.

- Make a list of the ways that you believe your customers can tell the difference between you and your competition.
- Other than product and price, what do you really sell? Make a list.
- Why would a customer pay for your product or service over and above your competition? Develop three reasons.
- What is your level of commitment to achieving organizational and individual distinction?

ONE

HOW WE GOT INTO THIS MESS:
THE THREE DESTROYERS OF DIFFERENTIATION

The moment was one of the most surreal that I have ever experienced. A farm kid from Crothersville, Indiana, I was part of a team invited by an international organization, People-to-People, to participate in a good-will mission. At home, the United States was in the midst of a presidential election between our only non-elected president and a peanut farmer from Georgia. It was our bicentennial year.

But that day I was standing in Red Square, in Moscow, in the Soviet Union—at the very center of communism.

Even though it was September, the day was unseasonably cold and gray. Behind my colleagues and me was the bland and massive GUM department store, occupying a significant space on Red Square. In front of us was the tomb of the father of communism, his body resting inside, appearing almost as a wax figure. Just beyond loomed the sight of the imposing Kremlin. The sentries at Lenin's Tomb goose-stepped their way through the changing of the guard in a manner that I had witnessed only in old black-and-white newsreel footage of the Nazi soldiers in Hitler's Germany. Their precision and efficiency were completely devoid of emotion.

As the ceremony silently concluded, a short, rotund senior citizen stopped me and asked in broken English if I was, in fact, an American. I affirmatively answered with pride in my country yet with a bit of fear as I was certainly in unfamiliar territory.

He opened his coat and pointed to a scar on his chest. With tears in his eyes, he gestured at his wound and said, "From war. Please! No war. No more war."

Wait, We're the Good Guys!

I was stunned. Like most Americans of that era, I assumed the Soviets were the aggressors, not us. Nevertheless, here was an obviously earnest Russian who firmly believed we were the enemy.

Slowly I assured him war was not our intent, and I hoped it wasn't the objective of his country either. I emphasized my colleagues and I were greatly enjoying our visit and were grateful to see his homeland. As someone standing beside him translated my English into his Russian, he broke into a wide, toothy smile and nodded rapidly in agreement.

Just a bit befuddled, I then asked him, "Out of this large crowd, how in the world could you recognize me as an American?"

He spoke to his friend, who then turned to me and said, "Your clothes have color. You are smiling, having fun, as you are in Red Square. That gave it all away."

The fact my clothes were not the standard-issue Soviet gray, and the fact that I seemed to be enjoying myself set me apart from the crowd. It pegged me as someone from another place.

It was a lesson in being *different*—the lesson of this book.

What I saw in the Soviet Union of the 1970s was the result of conformity and similarity, which is, historically, the natural occurence when the state owns or controls almost everything. The emphasis on uniformity seems to be a constant of every monolithic institution.

However, communism isn't the only political or economic doctrine that produces bland sameness. Ironically enough, capitalistic competition serves just as well.

To truly understand how to create distinction, it's first important to understand why distinction is so rare in today's marketplace. It's why this chapter focuses on the Three Destroyers that created the collapse of distinction.

Taken individually, each of these Three Destroyers of Differentiation creates a compelling challenge. When combined, they have a synergistic and destructive impact on your industry, your organization, and even upon you, professionally and personally, as well.

Differentiation Destroyer #1: Copycat Competition and Incremental Advancement

In our competitive, capitalistic society, the bar is continually going to be raised. We will naturally and constantly seek advantages for our products and services to move customers to choose us over the other guys and gals.

When you are faced with a competitive situation, you've got to constantly get better and provide more compelling reasons for your customers to spend money with you. Otherwise, you will go out of business. (This point shouldn't be surprising to anyone in business.)

However, here's the interesting and challenging rub that's often overlooked: When my competitor creates a point of differentiation and gains an advantage, my natural inclination is to either:

- merely imitate the competition's improvement, or
- attempt to incrementally improve upon the advancement.

If you get slightly ahead of me with a new advancement or strategy, my natural response is to replicate it. If I can discover a method to duplicate your effort, it then becomes easy for my customer base—and for the team inside our organization—to believe you no longer have a competitive advantage.

If your new method has enabled you to gain significant traction in the marketplace, then my best move appears to be to attempt to imitate whatever created your advantage and attempt to marginally do you one better.

In addition, I will probably call my latest effort the "new category leader," built to eliminate your advantage. For example, how many mobile phone manufacturers have been proclaiming their newest product to be the "iPhone killer"? (If we were in Vegas, we would ask, "What's the over/under on . . . *all* of them?")

Notice the problem: in both examples, all efforts are based upon what my *competitor* is doing, not necessarily what my *customers* desire. And in most cases, such advancements are evolutionary—not revolutionary.

Unfortunately, if I'm like executives in many industries, I am thinking I don't want to stick my neck out too far—because you may chop it off in front of our customers and prospects. (Since we are competitors, my customers are your prospects and vice versa.) You feel the same way. The result is incremental, uninspiring advancement that appears to be "safe."

In the long run, however, this approach is anything but safe! Instead, what we are doing is mutually destroying any points of differentiation that can better serve our customers and enhance our respective organizations.

It seems to me that the perfect model of capitalism is that you and I compete *for the customer*. These competitive efforts reduce costs—and therefore the price of our goods and services—while each of us also brings innovation to the marketplace

> *In the real world, it seems we focus upon competing against each other when instead we should be competing for the customer.*

that benefits the client. We continue to strive to meet the client's needs while, at the same time, we grow our respective organizations through the enhanced business we are achieving because of the superior value we are providing.

Yet, in almost every case in the real world, we instead compete *against each other.* Our focus seems to be directed toward others in the same industry that produce a similar product and deliver similar services, all the while playing the internal political games inherent within any organization.

It's not my desire to offend in any manner whatsoever. However, it is my belief that a significant factor in the demise of General Motors' position of global dominance was their laser-like focus upon the competition—the Toyotas, the BMWs, and so forth—as opposed to being absolutely obsessed with delivering what their *customers* REALLY wanted. And GM isn't the only automaker who's made this mistake. The traditional players watched one another so closely, it opened the door for newer entrants such as Hyundai and Kia to focus upon customers and make significant inroads into the market.

When Times Become Difficult

Add the element of a volatile economy, combined with more global competition than ever, and our desire is enhanced to play "follow the leader" with our competition. They cut staff; we do too. They close a location; we do too. They outsource a call center, and we're right behind them. All of us pull in our horns, hunker down, and attempt to ride out the busts.

It is simply overwhelming how many companies appear to be focused upon "not losing to the competition"—rather than on delivering what customers crave.

If you follow sports, you are familiar with the stories of the teams that lost important games because they played "not to lose." By going into the "prevent defense" too early in football or by slowing down the game and holding onto the ball in basketball, stellar teams have gotten out of the flow of the game and become so tense, they lost the ability to execute at their normal, highly skilled level of play.

Tennis professional and instructor Ron Waite makes an important distinction when discussing this phenomenon with his students. He tells them that playing "cautiously" is not the same as playing "smartly."[1]

The same point is almost always true in business. When we direct our focus toward the competition, we may become too cautious and seldom execute the smart strategy for winning and keeping customers.

Customers Raise Their Expectations

Customers also play a part in enforcing this kind of incremental advance. They too participate in the first Destroyer of Differentiation. It is part of the DNA, if you will, of our system that the competitive, capitalistic form of economics will also goad customers into steadily, methodically increasing their demands, no matter the economic climate.

The best explanation of why consumers take this approach comes from a close friend of mine, Dr. Michael LeBoeuf, the best-selling author of one of my favorite business books, *GMP: The Greatest Management Principle in the World.*

His principle is simply this: "Behavior rewarded is behavior repeated."[2]

Consider for a moment how that principle comes into play with regard to customer demands.

Behavior rewarded is behavior repeated, especially when it comes to escalating customer demands.

Here's an example from the automotive industry: if I work until five o'clock and the service department at your dealership closes at the same time, we both have a problem. I can't get my car serviced, and you can't get my business.

However, if your dealership responds to my situation by staying open additional hours, I am going to reward you with my business. Behavior rewarded is behavior repeated.

It's the first outcome, and it explains why businesses that are rewarded for superior customer service—for example, Nordstrom, Southwest and Virgin Airlines, Starbucks and Enterprise Rent-A-Car, to name a few—become even more focused on strategies that connect them with their customers. Happy customers return and spend more, so naturally the business serving them becomes more aware of the importance of creating those types of experiences because of the rewards of improved sales.

However, the second outcome is a bit less obvious. Because your organization has rewarded my demands as a customer in a manner I recognize to be positive from my perspective (I need extended hours for service, and you've accommodated my request), I will now intuitively feel compelled to make additional demands upon you.

You seem to prize my behavior of increasing my requirements for loyalty, because you've rewarded it; therefore, I—and the multitude of customers like me—will repeat it. It's like the humorous saying "No good deed goes unpunished!"

Why should I, your customer, just relax, content in my appreciation for a service bay that remains open until midnight? Because you have rewarded my request—behavior rewarded is behavior repeated—I'm going to replicate and enhance my expectations.

And, by the way, what *else* can you do for me?

Doing good means your customers will hasten their demand for you to do better!

Am I suggesting you should stop acquiescing to customer requests and demands? Of course not.

However, you need to understand two important points:

- Customer demands are always going to accelerate.
- This phenomenon is true for you—and your competition.

Therefore, since we are all confronted with a customer base that is accelerating its demands, and if your competition finds you have a point of competitive advantage, especially one that is perceived to be ongoing and sustainable, it is inherent in our system for them to:

- Imitate your advantage (as previously stated).
- Attempt to incrementally improve their product or service (mentioned earlier, as well).
- Or (and here's where a baby boomer like me should announce, "Danger, danger, Will Robinson!") they will cut their price to reduce your superior positioning.

A Dangerous Outcome

What occurs when neither you nor I can think of much more we can do to improve our product or service? What takes place when we do not know the formula to create distinction? What ensues when you have already imitated me as much as you can, and I have already done the same in imitation of you? Here's what happens:

1. You cut your price to develop some point of advantage.
2. I do the same to keep up with your discounting.
3. We both erode our profit margins, which means there are fewer resources for either of us to innovate and distinguish our efforts.
4. We corrode any distinction—and the related goodwill and

loyalty—customers perceive about our organization's products and services, which leads to a potential spiral of price pressures, which further diminishes any possibility that we will break the cycle.

As simple as this sounds, I often deal with companies—or management teams or sales forces—that wake up to discover they are on this treadmill with very little perspective on how they got there, and no strategy for how to extricate themselves.

And that's just the first of the Three Destroyers. Combine the impact of this first point with the next one.

Differentiation Destroyer #2: Change That Creates Tougher Competition

If you have not already read it, please allow me to recommend a highly compelling book: Eric Schlosser's *Fast Food Nation*.[3] After you digest (pardon the pun) his material, I'll wager you won't consume a hamburger for weeks. You may not agree with all the points Schlosser advocates, but I'll bet you cannot put his book aside.

While much of Schlosser's work does for the fast-food industry what Upton Sinclair did decades earlier for meatpacking in *The Jungle*, I find it highly interesting to view the early part of the book as a real historical examination of what transpired in our country from a cultural—as opposed to a dietary or culinary—perspective. Schlosser outlines how fast-food franchises exploded on the back of the Interstate Highway System. Distribution got easier, and so did copycat competition.

Businesses of every type, from department stores and electronics mega-centers to specialty coffee shops, multiplied in a frenzy of duplication and imitation. Schlosser basically traces the steps that ensured our nation would experience a collapse of distinction.

Taking the Adventure out of Lunch

"In my day," my dad would brag, "stopping for lunch was an adventure." He did not always mean that as a positive point.

Dad meant that as you traveled down a two-lane state or U.S. highway, you'd better keep an eye out for a diner where the truckers were eating. Believe it or not, the common belief at the time was that truckers, who were eating more meals on the road than the average American traveler, would naturally know the best places to dine.

As the son and grandson of truck drivers, I respectfully assert that I have absolutely no idea how our collective thinking became so twisted that those who hauled interstate commerce also became our pseudo-reliable sources of gastronomic expertise. Nonetheless, without a doubt, this accurately describes the thinking of the common person prior to the arrival and rapid expansion of the Interstate Highway System.

When those dual-lane, rapid-transit superhighways opened, travelers whisking down the interstate soon discovered they no longer had to endure the mysteries of Main Street U.S.A. Instead, the new generation of fast-driving travelers wanted to jump off an exit and fill up both their tanks and their stomachs.

I can still recall Dad's unique delight at the fact that every McDonald's was almost exactly identical. A Big Mac tasted the same no matter where you bought it. He quickly purchased cholesterol-on-a-sesame-seed-bun, ensured his kids remained relatively quiet and happy with their meals, and kept the pedal to the metal.

No one in our cramped Chevy dared to complain about the meal, because it was the very same lunch everyone had eaten and liked just fine yesterday, four hundred miles back up the road.

As both conventional wisdom and Schlosser suggest, the other chains that were simultaneously developing and expanding often did not have the wealth of capital on hand to execute the extensive site-selection procedures that became so scientific and strategic at McDonald's Corporation. So these competitors did the next best thing: they bought property as close to a McDonald's as possible to construct their next location. If the area was good enough for McDonald's, it had to be just fine, for example, for Burger King as well.

Instead of McDonald's having a monopoly on interstate highway exchanges, the corporation inadvertently pioneered a boom of investments in farmland plots slightly away from the Main Street commercial areas of the vast number of communities adjoining the interstate highway.

Seemingly in the blink of an eye, Alvie Kern of Crothersville—and thousands of small business owners just like him across the United States—was in serious economic trouble for the first time in his entrepreneurial life. He was confronted with competition he had never imagined in his wildest dreams. He was facing rivals that had barely existed, as far as he knew, just a few years earlier.

Put yourself in Alvie's shoes for a moment. You are not a businessperson, no matter what your hometown believes. You are a sandwich person.

This is a perfect example of a phenomenon of many organizations—and particularly small businesses. A guy starts a sporting goods store not because he sees an opening in the marketplace or a chance to be distinctive. Instead, he's a local jock who wants to stay involved in sports. I've done lots of work lately in the automotive body shop industry, meeting many owners of car repair shops who got into the business because they wanted to fix cars—not because of any particular business acumen.

Don't get me wrong: passion for your craft and significant knowledge of your industry is critical for any endeavor.

However—and this is a brutal fact—having a passion for what you do does not mean you will have a successful business.

Product knowledge and industry commitment is not enough. Something additional—something *distinctive*—is required if you are to cinch a triumph.

> *Having a passion for what you do does not mean you will have a successful business.*

Consider this: if you're Alvie Kern, you've always known how to make a great blue plate special, and that has always served you and your customers very well.

Now, however, your patrons can drive through a fast-food chain restaurant less than four miles down the road from you and still be back at work before you can get them and their greasy white bags of food out your front door.

I still remember Alvie constantly grousing in his cigarette-induced gravelly voice that he didn't understand how "anyone could eat that McDonald's junk"—all the while losing business to the chain in droves.

Now It's Not the Interstate—It's the Internet

In today's world in which you and I compete, it's not the interstate bringing new competition to us, as it did to the diner in my hometown—it's the Internet.

Your customer now has access to two factors that can make it very difficult for you to differentiate: competition and information.

In the past, if I wanted to purchase a bottle of aftershave, I would go to a bricks-and-mortar store in my city. There were a variety of retailers merchandising the product, from drugstores with Aqua Velva to department stores with Polo.

Now, however, all I need to do is go online, and I can select from a myriad of manufacturers and a plethora of products.

As an example, my favorite cologne is Chanel's Antaeus for Men. However, the fragrance was recently discontinued in the United States by Chanel, making it practically impossible for me to find it in any store in my home country, even as it remained on the market in much of the rest of the world.

No problem. I simply go to StrawberryNet.com, place my order, and it's shipped to my front door almost instantly. It's now, in many ways, easier for me to purchase my cologne from Hong Kong than where I used to buy it—the nearest Nordstrom in suburban Indianapolis.

The second aspect of how the Internet is destroying differentiation is perhaps even more challenging: customers now have access to an infinite amount of *information*.

As a "fanboy" of Apple—my very first computer was the Apple IIe, and I have never been without a Mac since they were introduced—I enthusiastically follow the company, which means I go to various "rumor sites" such as AppleInsider.com, MacRumors.com, TUAW.com (The Unofficial Apple Weblog), MacDailyNews.com (and there are literally dozens more) to keep up with the latest Apple news.

While of course many of the rumors about new products and innovations coming from Apple aren't always accurate, it amazes me to talk with employees at the Apple Stores around the country to discover that customers often know as much about what is in the Apple corporate pipeline as those at the Genius Bars do!

Today, when a customer walks onto a car lot to purchase a new or used vehicle, they frequently possess practically the same information as the salesperson with whom they will be negotiating. The customer may have accessed the dealer's price on the car, what incentive payments the dealership will receive, and even the history of the specific car she is considering for purchase. ("Show me the Carfax!") In other words, not only do customers have access to abundant information, they also can discover data that previously was confidential or proprietary within your organization.

And if a customer can obtain this input about you, so can your competition.

How do you compete? What do you do?

The Fatal Approach of the Nondifferentiated

If you were like most people in Alvie Kern's situation, your reaction to Destroyer #2—dynamic cultural, technological, and societal change delivering tough, new competitors to your doorstep—is to execute precisely the wrong strategy.

If you are a small-town diner owner like Alvie, you will erroneously tend to believe that your product is a hamburger. If you build the better burger, you assume that you will become the better burger business once again.

Many of your customers are now going to McDonald's—so your natural response is to try to "out-McDonald's" the competition and restore your hometown business.

Unfortunately, in almost every situation, despite your best intentions, you cannot out-original the initial player.

Fast-food chains have obviously proliferated—but why?

The key to the success of other franchises was to build upon McDonald's efforts at consistency, *and to find specific points of differentiation* that enabled them to obtain their unique places in the market.

Therefore, flame-broiled or 100 percent fresh (not frozen) beef or roast beef sandwiches or tacos, rather than burgers, succeeded, while the outmatched local diner often did not.

"But wait a minute," you may be thinking. "Your hometown establishment *did* have points of differentiation. It had a local, engaged proprietor who poured his—and his family's—heart and soul into the business. You've already pointed out it had a unique taste and atmosphere. Wasn't that enough?"

No, it wasn't. And the reason why leads us to Destroyer #3.

Differentiation Destroyer #3: Familiarity Breeds Complacency

One adage I heard often from my mom was "Familiarity breeds contempt."

As much as I hate to dispute my mother's advice, my experience has taught me this one isn't true. Becoming more familiar with someone does not automatically guarantee that you will become contemptuous of him or her.

When something like a product or service is present to the point that it becomes thoroughly familiar and is boundlessly available, we do not then begin to scorn it, hate it, or express disdain toward it.

Instead, we begin to take it for granted. We become complacent and presume it will always be around.

We see this all the time in our personal lives. Unfortunately, we take for granted the people who are closest to us. We don't intend disrespect toward our spouses, for example. However, a steady drift toward complacency just seems to be a part of the human makeup.

Perhaps we presuppose that if something or someone is overwhelmingly familiar, it represents a garden we no longer need to tend as enthusiastically or systematically. We erroneously assume, for example, that the love of our spouse will always be there on the vine, and it doesn't require as much nurturing, intensity, or the commitment of time that is demanded by something that we have yet to acquire.

Taking It for Granted

This phenomenon was a significant problem for Kern's Grill. Our family often went there for lunch, so we took it for granted. To try someplace new—like McDonald's then, and perhaps your competitor now—was fun, different, and therefore exciting.

It honestly never occurred to us that because the members of our family went to McDonald's a few times a week—instead of Kern's Grill—Alvie's business would be so severely affected.

But it was.

The reason is obvious. Just as we felt our slight shift in patronage would not cause a seismic economic change in the grill's fortunes, neither did others in town believe they possessed so much clout.

However, when a portion of the McKains' business at Kern's Grill—as well as the business of just about every other family like us in town—was subtracted, a significant segment of the revenues of one little family diner was erased. It never crossed our minds that we were murdering a business, and we even owned a small establishment across the street.

This phenomenon of business psychology has fascinated me for years. Business owners do not think like business owners when they are customers someplace else. They think like customers.

Salespeople do not think like salespeople when they are shopping. They think like customers.

When a cowboy purchases a trailer to haul his horses, he doesn't think and relate to the dealership selling him that trailer like an agricultural businessperson, even though he fills that role for his ranch during his working hours. He thinks like a customer.

When a CEO buys a new BMW, she doesn't think and relate to the dealership selling her that new 7-Series like a CEO, even though she fills that role for her company every day. She thinks like a customer.

When we are the customer, we all assume the customer position.

Conversely, the same is often true in the attitude of a business toward its loyal customers. When we are running our businesses and doing our jobs, we think like professionals—and, unfortunately, often fail to think like the customer.

Perhaps this phenomenon explains an aspect of business I believe is impossible to rationalize once it is recognized: we tend to pursue new customers with more enthusiasm than we prize existing ones.

In my book *What Customers REALLY Want,* I write that every organization or professional on the planet has some kind of *acquisition strategy*; in other words, almost all of us have some kind of specific plan for attracting new customers.

However, few companies or professionals have a *retention strategy*, a precise program that outlines specific steps for retaining our current customers, for growing and expanding the business we are obtaining from them.[4]

Once again, the example of our personal lives is the perfect metaphor for customer retention and growth.

Every marriage counselor will agree that an excellent approach for enhancing a relationship is to continue to romance the person who has already committed his or her life to you.

When we are dating, we take all of the steps necessary to encourage the relationship. We make phone calls and send flowers, cards, or e-mails. We try to surprise our loved one with little efforts that are out of the ordinary and above and beyond normal dating. Unfortunately, it all ends at "I do" for many couples.

Why is that true? I honestly don't know, and I'm not really qualified

> *We tend to pursue new customers with more enthusiasm than we prize existing ones.*

to speculate. The late Jim Rohn, a famed business philosopher, simply called it "one of the mysteries of the mind." It is just the way most people are. Rohn advises that, rather than excessively ponder and attempt to discover the reasons for this behavioral abnormality at length, we should instead do something more productive—accept this behavior as fact, then hold ourselves to a higher standard than the masses.[5]

What Did Kern's Grill Do?

Had Kern's Grill been more customer-focused prior to the advent of drive-through fast food, perhaps the diner could have survived the McDonald's onslaught. However, because it wasn't truly differentiated, and because the owners took their customers for granted then lamely tried to imitate the hot new competitors, they were caught in the collapse of distinction.

Kern's Grill died a relatively quick death in Crothersville.

Alvie Kern just didn't have the capital to make the strategic business investments that might have created the differentiation the restaurant needed to survive. Frankly, he probably did not possess the business acumen to do so, even if he had the cash.

As I recall, he basically stated he was closing the restaurant for "health reasons." As my dad said—with more than a slight bit of newfound fear regarding how quickly fortunes could change for any business owner in the face of new competition—the health problem was probably the fact that losing his business was killing him.

WIIFU—What's in It for Us?

What does the demise of a greasy spoon diner in a small town have to do with your organization? Well, *everything*.

Do you think it happens only to insignificant businesses in undersized markets? Think again!

Consider the world of retailing—not just in a solitary small town, but also throughout America.

Then picture yourself as Montgomery Ward's.

Aaron Montgomery Ward created what was perhaps the first mail-order corporation in 1872, with an innovative, single-sheet catalog offering 163 items. Additionally, he earned recognition as the first national retailer in the United States to create a "satisfaction guaranteed" offer for his customers.[6] This superior service and an impressive assortment of quality goods at affordable prices led to rapid growth.

What do you imagine Aaron Montgomery Ward thought about when, back in 1886, fourteen years after Ward's founding, Richard W. Sears started a business in Minneapolis selling watches to fellow train stationmasters through his company, which was initially known as the R. W. Sears Watch Company?

My guess is that Mr. Sears wasn't even on the radar screen (especially since radar screens weren't invented until many decades later).

Continue your rapid progression through mass-market retail history to the time a small business in Bentonville, Arkansas, entered the same fray.

Do you believe at first that the esteemed and highly compensated executive team at Sears even gave this upstart a second thought at that point?

"Come on," you can imagine them saying in the halls of their extravagant corporate headquarters, "their leader is a hick named Walton who drives a pickup. That company's not going to be a player on our field."

And if you are sitting now in the midst of that Arkansas empire, I suggest you should be wondering what you must figure out to prevent this Destroyer of Differentiation from doing to your organization what Sears did to Wards—and you did to Sears.

If you are Microsoft, you probably can't stand Google. Sony has to just hate Apple for what the iPod—and later the iPhone—did to the formerly dominant Walkman. The cycle continues on and on.

It is, to some degree, the pattern of disruptive innovation that Dr. Clayton Christensen brilliantly revealed in his landmark book *The Innovator's Dilemma* (Harvard Business Review Press, 1997).

Yet it is a bit more than that, as well. It's not exclusively an advance in technology that is creating the predicament in the cases we are examining. (The subtitle of Christensen's book is *When New Technologies Cause Great Firms to Fail*.) It wasn't that Walmart found a way to "out-technology" Sears. (Southwest Airlines disrupted its industry; however, the technology of the planes they fly has almost zero variation from those of the competition.)

It's that "great" just isn't good enough anymore. It's how you look at your business . . . and how customers see the difference, *if any*, between you and the competition.

Creating distinction for your business is imperative—not just to acquire space in today's marketplace from the competitors you are already encountering every day.

It's also vital because the future will undoubtedly mean your customers will be considering new competitors of whom you are not yet aware.

Consider this amalgamation of challenges:

- Constantly elevating demands of customers
- A volatile economy
- More competitors than ever in many industries, combined with the fact that, regardless of the specific field, your competition is now far easier for your customers and prospects to access
- Customers with more information than ever before, including

facts and figures that were previously proprietary and often secret

- Your best customers taking you for granted—and vice versa

How could you possibly consider doing business in today's economic and competitive climate *without* being distinctive?

Creating distinction in your market—and starting now—is vital in creating the future you want for your organization in today's hyper-competitive global economy.

The great news is that you can employ strategies that will build distinction immediately.

The goal of this book is to show you how to begin.

Executive Summary

I. There are Three Destroyers of Differentiation

   A. Each has had a powerful impact upon organizations and individual careers.

   B. Their synergistic impact is much more significant for you and your organization.

II. Differentiation Destroyer #1: Copycat Competition and Incremental Advancement

   A. Our capitalistic system ideally should produce a competitive environment in which we have to continually improve and provide compelling reasons for customers to do business with us because our competition will be doing the same thing.

   B. In the real world, we have been doing something different.

   C. If my competition creates a point of differentiation, my natural tendency is to:

      1. Imitate or even replicate that advancement.

      2. Incrementally improve upon that advancement.

   D. When we focus on what our competitor is doing, we center our activity on the competition rather than on the customer. We compete against each other rather than for the customer.

   E. We are also essentially executing only *evolutionary* advancements, rather than the *revolutionary* ones that true differentiation requires.

   F. When economic times become more challenging, we tend to pull in our horns and ride out the recession.

      1. This usually means we provide less of what our customers really want, and our competition does the same thing.

      2. The result is dissatisfied customers who spend less with all of us, in part because they cannot tell the difference between any of us.

III. Differentiation Destroyer #2: Change That Creates Tougher Competition

A. During the second half of the twentieth century, the Interstate Highway System provided new and faster connections between U.S. communities.

1. It also accelerated the speed of growth of fast-food restaurants and chain retailers.

2. As these new businesses appeared, entrenched local retailers were confronted with new competition they barely knew existed a short time earlier.

B. Local retailers often adopted the wrong strategy as they attempted to replicate the perceived advantages of the dynamic new competitor. (Given Destroyer #1, this was a predictable response.)

C. They usually discovered that if their competition was McDonald's, for example, they could not "out-McDonald's" the original.

D. Only through the development of specific points of differentiation can a business establish a unique place in the market.

1. Many retailers—steeped primarily in product knowledge and possessing a smaller degree of marketing and finance acumen—were not up to this challenge.

2. In most cases, customers chose the new—and differentiated— option, which, of course, often resulted in the demise of the non-differentiated competitor.

IV. Differentiation Destroyer #3: Familiarity Breeds Complacency

A. It is not what we were told as kids—familiarity does not breed contempt.

B. When we have become familiar with something and it is boundlessly available, we do not scorn it, hate it, or hold it in contempt. Instead, we take it for granted.

C. When we take something for granted, we no longer play as active a part in its growth and cultivation.

D. When that happens in personal and professional relationships, the association often wilts and dies for lack of attention.

E. When that impact is multiplied for a business across a wide range of customers, the result can be fatal for the company.

V. The impact of these Destroyers can be felt in every organization.

A. While a prevailing case study in this book is a small-town diner, the fact is that practically every organization is suffering from the synergistic impact of these Three Destroyers of Differentiation.

B. Here's the fundamental question: How can a business consider facing today's challenging economic climate without striving to attain differentiation?

C. The goal of this book is to show you how it is done.

Action Steps, Questions, and Ideas

- How have you imitated your competitors? How have they copied you?
  - Develop a list.
- What new competition has technology delivered to your doorstep?
  - What is your strategy to combat it?
- Where are your customers most familiar with your organization?
  - Are they so familiar that they have become bored?

TWO

WHO MOVED MY . . . CAREER?

"Why is it so much easier to lay off factory workers than any other employees?" a manager rhetorically asked me with a smirk.

I shook my head—in part because I didn't know the answer he was seeking, and in part because I couldn't believe he would ask such an insensitive question.

"Because," the manager continued, "there are just so darn many of them, and they are all so much alike."

Stunned at his crassness, I had to admit he was somewhat correct, nevertheless. A company can eradicate elements that are indistinguishable much more easily than it can cut a component that generates a recognizable difference.

If an employee in Bangalore can produce a product or service no different from one made or performed in Baltimore, why wouldn't an organization seeking to maximize profitability go with the least expensive alternative?

(Don't misunderstand: I realize there are all kinds of social implications and other sensitive issues surrounding this question. However, please notice the perspective from which it is being asked—a company seeking to do nothing but maximize bottom-line profitability.)

No matter your occupation, you are threatened by the failure of organizations to create distinction.

While we can understand the organization's decision from the standpoint of a "case study," it is one heck of a lot different when the job that is eliminated is *ours*. When the challenges and pressures brought upon organizations from the phenomenon we are discussing create personal impact, it accelerates our need for understanding. It leaves us wondering not just about "who moved my cheese"—we are dismayed someone or something has moved our entire career.

This chapter will change our focus from the effect of this phenomenon upon organizations and begin to examine the insidious influence of the Three Destroyers of Differentiation on your career . . . and you.

Examining Examples

To illustrate these challenges, let's pick a couple of areas of concentration, understanding these are merely metaphors for the peril in which we all find ourselves.

Let's assume you are a financial adviser. You care about your clients and their goals and dreams. Nevertheless, just when you thought your business was going to start becoming a little bit easier—since your ongoing tenure should mean a continually larger and growing book of business—it seems someone came along and changed all the rules.

You cannot figure out what happened. You went to seminars and improved your business and yourself a little bit every single year. Yet clients now seem bored or distracted when you bring them in for their semi-annual reviews. And when you are home on a Sunday afternoon watching your favorite NFL team, you can't help getting a little edgy at the parade of commercials for E*Trade, Charles Schwab, Scottrade, and other brokers promoting online tools for investing.

Your firm compensates you, in part, for obtaining new assets to manage and for the acquisition of new households of affluent investors for the firm. However, both are becoming harder to attract, not just because new competitors steer prospects away from you or because of volatility in the market. It's also because you are having a more difficult time keeping your current clients in the fold. Sometimes those clients are husbands and wives with whom you have had a long association; other times it's the sons and daughters who inherited the money you worked so hard to successfully invest.

And the impact isn't solely professional. It has become so much more difficult, you aren't having fun anymore.

The dramatic financial events of recent times may mean the firm where you work has been acquired by a competitor or is in danger of collapse as an institution altogether. You are always looking over your shoulder, wondering when the next client may go away. If the market trends downward, you retreat into hiding, fearing that if you contact your clients, they may move their accounts elsewhere. Yet, somewhere deep inside, you also realize that if you fail to call them, they may think you don't really care about their business and may move their accounts elsewhere.

Another Example

Now let's assume you are the owner of a small business, much like my parents with our grocery store or Alvie Kern with his diner. Perhaps without even realizing it, you face challenges similar to those of a financial adviser.

Let's say you are working hard to own and manage the best independent dry cleaner in your midsize city. You've upgraded the interiors of your stores, you've become more environmentally sensitive regarding the chemicals used, and you pride yourself on the care you give your customers' clothes.

Yet when the competitor located down the street cuts the price on shirts to $1.99, some of your customers choose them, instead. You are hurt and a bit upset. You attended the trade association meeting every year and learned the latest techniques and approaches in your industry. No one would argue with you that you are the best dry cleaner in town, but your business isn't growing.

You start noticing all the advertisements for fabric steamers at department stores. They claim that if you steam your suits and dresses, you won't have to pay to dry-clean them as often. Now—all of a sudden, it seems—your competition includes not only the cleaners down the street but mega-retailers such as Target as well.

So you let a couple of people go and work longer hours yourself, trying to keep your overhead reasonable. Some longtime customers ask you in a whisper if "anything's wrong" because they're concerned about your health, and others seldom come in. You are more tired and cranky than ever before, and you wonder whether you really should have sold insurance or real estate instead of opening a dry-cleaning establishment.

The Three Destroyers are already at work undermining your business. Here's how:

Destroyer #1: Copycat Competition and Incremental Advancement

You envisioned that keeping pace with the competition would enable you to be close to the local apex of your profession. That's Destroyer #1.

You always felt your competitors were the other financial advisers at your office—certainly, no more than the ones at the other local firms. Or if you are the entrepreneur, you could keep your eye on your rival because he was the other dry cleaner down the block. Therefore, you executed only incremental improvements, not significant ones that would create distinction.

If a competing financial adviser had a client meeting around a wine tasting and it received positive reviews, you did exactly the same. Maybe you even stepped it up a modest amount, hired the sommelier from a good local restaurant, and had a tasting just a bit more sophisticated than that of your rival at the other financial firm.

If the dry cleaner down the street offered same-day service, you did too. If he advertised "In by 9:00—out by 5:00," you put up a sign that stated "In by 9:30—out by 4:30," because you believed it would give you an advantage.

Were you inspired to change your practice or your business in a dramatic manner? Of course not. You didn't reconstruct your client base, nor did you become innovative.

Instead, you did one of the following:

- emulated your competitors so they couldn't achieve significant competitive differentiation, or
- delivered what you perceived to be the minimum degree of advancement required in order to establish yourself over your competitor as the primary provider of the goods and services inherent in your profession.

Here is the problem: neither strategy creates distinction.

- The first—*imitation*—merely does enough to keep your competitors in check. It does not create space in the marketplace; all it does is temporarily ensure that the pack of nondifferentiated competitors keeping their doors open will include you.
- The second—*incremental improvement*—maintains your positioning but fails to create the type of distinction that inspires the passion that results in client loyalty and engagement.

The Wisdom of . . . a Wrestler?

Ric Flair is a longtime star in professional wrestling. His real name is Richard Morgan Fliehr, and the "Nature Boy" (his nickname) was born in February 1949.

I mention when he was born to suggest that if someone can be over sixty years old and maintain significant success in his chosen profession, and still, to this day, occasionally climb in the ring wearing nothing more than glorified Speedo trunks—while possessing a somewhat less-than-glorious physique—and be cheered by thousands of adoring young fans—well, maybe, just maybe, he has a little something to say we should consider.

I discovered a nugget of wisdom in his autobiography, which I noticed at a bookstore one day. It's a no-nonsense component of the philosophy that creates differentiation: "To *be* the man . . . you gotta *beat* the man!"[1]

While Ric Flair has retired from the ring several times, only to repeatedly return, and while several allegations have recently been made that may bring his personal character into question, there is no doubt he still makes an important point you and I should consider.

Every professional I know will say they want to *be* the man—or the woman—who is highly successful. Yet few want to beat the man to achieve that goal. They want to play along with the man or tie the man or edge out the man. They usually desire to do nothing more than achieve approximate equality with "the man."

In other words, many seek only to execute the least progressive, most conforming activity they can to achieve a modest version of the success they desire.

They choose to walk the traditional path instead of taking Robert

Frost's legendary "road not taken" to get to where they want to go in life and in work. They want to triumph by a trivial margin, when true builders of distinction are never satisfied with the incremental.

Truly distinctive players want to *beat* "the man" so soundly, the competitor is no longer even considered.

So, the question becomes: how important is it to you to be differentiated . . . to create distinction . . . to be "*the* man" or "*the* woman"?

Focusing Upon Internal Competition

In the previous chapter, we explored how an organization that focuses more on the competition than their customers is likely to fall prey to this Destroyer. A similar phenomenon could be at play with your career internally, as well. The only thing worse than focusing on your competitor more than your customer is focusing more on internal adversaries than external challengers.

In the August 2012 issue of *Vanity Fair*, contributing editor Kurt Eichenwald related the story of Microsoft's use of a method to determine employee performance called "stack ranking."

"Every current and former Microsoft employee I interviewed— *every one*—cited stack ranking as the most destructive process inside of Microsoft, something that drove out untold numbers of employees," Eichenwald writes. "If you were on a team of 10 people, you walked in the first day knowing that, no matter how good everyone was, 2 people were going to get a great review, 7 were going to get mediocre reviews, and 1 was going to get a terrible review," says a former Microsoft software developer. "It leads to employees focusing on competing with each other rather than competing with other companies." [2]

In the article, Eichenwald inquires of former Microsoft engineer Brian Cody whether performance reviews were ever based on the quality of his work. Cody responded, "It was always much less about how I could become a better engineer and much more about my need to improve my visibility among other managers." Ed McCahill, a Microsoft marketing manager for sixteen years, says, "You look at the Windows Phone and you can't help but wonder, How did Microsoft squander the lead they had with the Windows CE devices? They had a great lead, they were years ahead. And they completely blew it. And they completely blew it because of the bureaucracy."[3]

If you're in an organization where your primary concern is competing with internal colleagues rather than for the business of external customers and prospects, you've got big problems.

Destroyer #2: Change That Creates Tougher Competition

Guess what? You have new competition knocking (electronically or in person) on your clients' doors. This creates an even more difficult challenge for you, in part because of your response to Destroyer #1.

Because you failed to create an innovative approach to the way you deal with your clients—and because you evaluated your success against a band of bland brothers and sisters in the profession or industry—your customers have stopped seeing how your specific involvement in their financial affairs or dry cleaning is bringing any significant value to their lives.

If a client doesn't feel you offer exceptional value or a compelling experience, why shouldn't they make inexpensive online trades or steam the dress at home?

Clients will always find a point of distinction. Therefore, if you fail to outline one for them in compelling fashion, they will go to the worst possible distinguisher for you: price.

Don't Live by the Price Sword

Price is no safe harbor against the constant pressure of competition. Everyone is vulnerable to it, both the innovators of yesterday and every business of today, because price knows no brand. It is not loyal to a community or a company or a history.

This means price is no friend of distinction. Discount brokerages, to continue our financial services example, are discovering this for themselves. In *USA Today*, reporter Matt Krantz wrote:

> Upstart online brokerages, such as Zecco.com, and aggressive banks, such as Wells Fargo and Bank of America, are giving the big four online brokerages—E-Trade, TD Ameritrade, Charles Schwab and Scottrade—a run for their money, and for yours, with offers of free online trades.
>
> "There are competitive pressures on the larger players," says James Lohmann, senior director at J. D. Power, a company that rates online brokerages. "Everyone has gotten cheaper," says Kurt Feierabend, 38, a consultant in Minneapolis who has had an account with TD Ameritrade and is looking to switch to a broker with lower fees.[4]

Go back and reread the customer's comment. Mr. Feierabend does not indicate that he is dissatisfied in any manner with TD Ameritrade. Instead, he is looking to switch so he can pay lower fees than those with the previously lower-priced brokerage. Which, of course, makes sense for him—and is horrible news for TD Ameritrade.

I guess we could say, "Live by the price sword, die by the price sword." TD Ameritrade and the other major online brokers mentioned in the article launched their businesses with discount trading as their distinguishing characteristic over the Merrill Lynch, UBS, Morgan Stanley types of firms. Now these Web-based discounters find themselves confronted with the challenge of Destroyer #2.

Entrepreneurs face similar challenges. To continue our independent business example, consider what Andrea Holecek wrote in the *Munster Times:* "Linda Dygert, who owns Valparaiso's Mercury Cleaners with her husband, Norm, said for someone just starting in the business . . . [it] could be a nightmare. The Dygerts have owned their business since they bought it from his father in 1982." Mrs. Dygert states in the article:

> The biggest challenge is trying to be competitive and do the right thing. But I wouldn't recommend anyone getting into the business. My husband works six days a week. On the seventh day he does maintenance. He gets up at 5 [a.m. and] leaves the business at 5:30 [p.m.] when it closes. So there are very long hours and huge commitments. And you're never out of debt because you always have to buy new equipment.[5]

I'm certain the Dygerts do a terrific job. However, on a generic basis, have you ever done business at a place where the owner loves her job and you can just *tell*?

On the other hand, have you patronized stores where you can easily intuit that the owners are trapped and wouldn't wish their business *or* their lives on anyone? Do they ever take out their frustrations on their ever-dwindling number of customers?

No matter what your field, you will experience competitive pressures. What will your response be? What will you do?

Here's a tip: it had better not involve the lowest price.

Yet you also have to wonder—in the cases of both the small dry cleaner and the financial adviser, as they deal with these Destroyers of Differentiation—what they are feeling about their longtime customers. And how do these longtime customers now feel about them?

Destroyer #3: Familiarity Breeds Complacency

Your customers are bored, and I'll bet you never saw it coming.

You bring in your clients for their annual reviews, let them know your performance beat the market average by 4 percent, fill them in on new investments you have discovered that are congruent with their preferred approaches and risk tolerances, and you can almost see their eyes glaze over.

How in the world could they be bored when you are talking about something so important?

Your clients are bored because familiarity breeds complacency.

Think this is an isolated phenomenon? Hardly. As Joe Edwards reported in *Nation's Restaurant News* all the way back in 1984, Brock Hotel Corporation, the parent company of a chain of restaurants, was struggling with the choices needed to solve the problems created by customer boredom. Customer boredom was "a real problem," and fighting it was critical to the chain's success.

What was boring the customers? Believe it or not, ShowBiz Pizza. The stores consisted of teen dance centers with a $20,000 package (in 1984 dollars) of disco lights, dance floor, and sound equipment, as well as one-hundred-seat theaters featuring dazzling films, such as a twenty-three-minute movie with special effects created by Douglas Trumbull, the cinematic genius who worked on several major motion pictures including *Close Encounters of the Third Kind*.[6]

Now, if *that* is boring to customers, what can you do to excite them? (And it bears mentioning those adolescent customers in 1984 are now, more than a quarter-century later, your adult customers.)

For another example, customers never call the phone company to say "thanks" simply because they have a dial tone. I have never called my cable TV company to tell them I appreciate the extraordinary speed with which I can access the Internet because of their connection in my home. We take these truly amazing pieces of technological delivery for granted.

As *The Grocer* reported in its October 2005 edition, "Grocery shopping has become so boring that some consumers are more excited by the nonfood in their supermarkets, according to new IGD research."[7] Yet grocery shopping today offers more choices, convenience, and experience than ever before.

Like it or not, customers are going to treat your efforts with similar ennui. If customers know your routine almost as well as you do, you have substantial problems.

What have you changed in the past year in your approach to your customers?

If your answer is "basically nothing," it begs the question: what makes *you* different?

The Trifecta

Wow! What a combination you have going for you:

1. You are creating only incremental improvements so nothing really distinguishes you from your competition in any meaningful fashion.
2. You are encountering new competitors you didn't even dream of a few years earlier—tough, price-slashing competitors that can rapidly deliver either a similar or the very same product or service to your customers.

3. You are taken for granted by the customers you have served for years because they have been lulled into complacency through their total familiarity with your execution.

What can you do?

Now that you understand what has created the collapse of distinction—from both organizational and individual standpoints—in the next chapter we will take a look at what creates differentiation in the marketplace.

It's important to note that differentiated does not equal distinctive. However, differentiation is the first place you need to stop on your journey to create the distinction that is vital to your individual and organizational success. It's a critical point, whether you are an executive at a global conglomerate, a professional seeking greater success, or even an entrepreneur running a small-town diner.

Executive Summary

I.   The Three Destroyers of Differentiation have an impact that is not limited to corporations.

    A. Their destructive impact is also felt by individual professionals trying to survive and thrive in their careers.

    B. No matter your occupation, you are threatened by the collapse of distinction.

II. Examining examples

    A. Financial services: Just when you thought you'd have a larger and growing book of business you could easily maintain by matching the efforts of your competition, your clients seem bored and distracted; they're seeking less costly online alternatives; it's harder to retain them and obtain new clients; and in today's market, it's no fun on a personal basis anymore.

    B. Retail dry cleaners: You've upgraded your stores and become environmentally conscious, yet when your competition cuts their price, you do too. You're working harder (for less money) and not enjoying it at all.

    C. What has created these problems? The Three Destroyers of Differentiation.

III. The impact of the Three Destroyers on individual professionals

    A. Destroyer #1: Copycat Competition and Incremental Advancement

        1. You believed that by keeping pace with your competition, you would stay in the game.

        2. Therefore, you emulated what they did—and they did the same in response to what you did.

        3. The problem is that neither of you are now differentiated in any meaningful way from the other.

4. The Ric Flair example: "To *be* the man . . . you've got to *beat* the man." Most professionals take the least progressive, most conforming activity possible to achieve a minimally acceptable level of success.

B. Destroyer #2: Change That Creates Tougher Competition

1. New competitors, arriving on your doorstep because of technological advances—from the Interstate Highway System to the Internet—are creating new challenges.

2. If you have felt the impact of Destroyer #1, the dilemma presented by Destroyer #2 is exacerbated.

a. Not only are you non-differentiated from your existing competition, but now there are new players in the game offering lower costs or faster or cheaper service.

b. And if you've lived by the "price sword," you may now find that you are going to perish from it as well.

C. Destroyer #3: Familiarity Breeds Complacency

1. Because "familiarity breeds complacency," if you approach customers in the same personal manner you have used in the past, they are becoming bored with your approach and technique.

2. What have you changed in the past year in your approach to customers?

a. If you can't think of an answer, then the response should be "nothing."

IV. The Trifecta: You have discovered the intense personal impact of the Three Destroyers of Differentiation.

A. You are creating only incremental improvement, if any at all.

B. You are encountering new competition you did not anticipate.

C. You are taken for granted by your customers because you have lulled them into complacency.

Action Steps, Questions, and Ideas

- Name specific stages in your career when the Destroyers of Differentiation have affected you.

- Do you want to be "the man" or "the woman"? Are you willing to beat "the man" to get there? Or are you content with achieving "good enough" status? Write a paragraph that explains your position, your intentions, and two action steps you will take.

- What have you changed in the past year to freshen your approach with your customers and colleagues?

THREE

THREE LEVELS OF DIFFERENTIATION

In the all-time classic film comedy from 1978, *National Lampoon's Animal House*, there is a statue at the legendary Faber College in Faber, Pennsylvania. Placed in front of the administration building, which houses the office of the evil Dean Vernon Wormer (played to perfection by the late John Vernon), is a sculpture of the college's founder, the lead-pencil tycoon Emil Faber. Inscribed on the pedestal is the motto of this esteemed institution: *Knowledge is good.*

Okay, I admit that I have a weird sense of humor, and that little witticism made me laugh out loud.

It seems all institutions of higher learning, though, have mottos. At Harvard, for example, the phrase is *Veritas* (Latin for "truth").

At Yale, evidently as an example of the phenomenon we cited earlier of imitating your competitor while attempting incremental improvement, the motto is *Lux et veritas* ("light and truth").

Die Luft der Freiheit weht is Stanford's unofficial motto and translates from the German as "the wind of freedom blows." (The phrase is a quote from Ulrich von Hutten, a sixteenth-century humanist, as reported on the official Stanford website.)

My friend, Dr. Nido Qubein, is president of the rapidly growing High Point University in High Point, North Carolina. (I'll use HPU later as a brilliant example of creating distinction in the crowded marketplace of higher education.) The institution over which he presides is directed by the phrase *Nil sine numine* (Latin for "nothing without divine guidance").

However, the illustrious (and fictional) Faber College affirms the pseudo-profound statement *Knowledge is good*.

In this chapter we'll examine a small portion of the theory behind three primary strategies for creating differentiation. These are concepts that I believe will provide significant light and truth because, at the end of the day, "differentiation is good." (And much, much more!)

Leaders of organizations are employed to select and direct the strategies they believe will make their businesses more profitable. I hope you are beginning to see that no one can afford to overlook differentiation and still maintain any kind of competitive lead, regardless of the size of the business or the industry it's part of.

But first, what is *differentiation*? And is it different from *distinction*?

There is a lot of literature and discussion using these words, but what exactly do they mean? Since both terms are used here—and treated somewhat interchangeably—it might be easy to get confused. There is some overlap in meaning, after all.

Both terms mean you have created clear advantages over your competition in the marketplace. Both terms mean that you are executing strategies—individually or organizationally—that will either establish or maintain your ability to display to your customers and colleagues that they should prefer what you offer. Therefore, either term can mean the effort to set you and your organization apart from your competitors in a cluttered marketplace.

Where these terms differ, as they will be used here, is in their *degree*. I'm suggesting they fall at different places along a continuum.

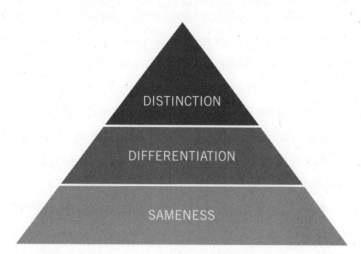

Level one is *sameness*, that "sea of similarity" my old-timer friend back home was discussing. This is the place where most organizations—and, frequently, the professionals who work for them—are found adrift. It does not necessarily mean their product doesn't work or their service is lousy. It's that they do not have the requisite characteristics that would compel their customers to be loyal and passionate about their products or services. They are the ones who become the casualties of the Three Destroyers of Differentiation we discussed earlier.

Level two is *differentiation*. Businesses and workers at this level are not satisfied with numbing similarity, so they display characteristics to set them apart from their competition. They will point to various aspects of their products and services and say, "See! This proves we are better than our rivals!" Beware, though: the unique points of which the organization is so proud may not find traction with customers.

In my consulting business, I endlessly hear from organizations directing me to their "friendly customer service" as being a point of differentiation—and, of course, their competitors claim exactly the same thing!

If both you and your competition prove uniqueness by referring to identical characteristics, then neither of you is correct. This approach creates no point of advantage from the customer's perspective. You are the same.

And just being "different" does not secure true "differentiation."

If I slap every customer in the face, I may be truly "different" from my competition, but have I obtained any goodwill from my customers, prospects, and colleagues that will enhance my business?

Level three is *distinction*. Because of the collapse we discussed in chapter one, this level is an extraordinarily rare place for individuals and organizations to reside. Nevertheless, we all know professionals or companies who become the "go to" provider in any—and just about every—industry. They are so uncommonly excellent, or their differentiation strategies are executed to such an extraordinary level of precision, that these distinct examples become clear market leaders.

Consider the computer industry—specifically the laptop market—and you can come up with a lot of names at level one (sameness) with relative ease.

These manufacturers all seem to run together in a pack of similarity. Asus, Gateway, Hitachi, Acer, and Fujitsu, among others, come to mind in the laptop market. I'm certain they all make a fine product, and I know they usually charge a lower price.

> *Just being different does not secure true differentiation or distinction.*

But it is difficult for me to find an exceptionally compelling reason to choose an Acer over an Asus, as a case in point, because I'm just not aware of any specific points that would assist me in discriminating between them.

Level two (differentiation) are those manufacturers that are known for something: HP laptops are media centers; Dell is built-to-order on a budget; Sony integrates their line of digital still and video cameras and other products into their Vaio units. Level two manufacturers all possess their unique points of differentiation and so attempt to justify why you, the prospective customer, might choose to not only purchase a Sony as opposed to an Asus but also potentially be prepared to spend more to acquire it.

As a customer, I walk into the store *assuming* I'm probably going to have to spend a few extra dollars to get a Sony instead of an Asus. That's the power of differentiation, and it generates the perception that purchasing an HP laptop, for example, is a superior choice and value than selecting a product from a company operating at level one, even though level one manufacturers have a worthwhile product they sell at a lower price.

Level three (distinction) is best represented by Apple and its line of MacBooks. The Mac has become, to use the term of author and consultant Joe Calloway, a "category of one." The Mac has developed to the extent that it no longer merely possesses points of differentiation; it has risen to a class all its own.

In fact, according to research from the NPD Group, of all laptop computers sold above the $1,000 price point, Apple's line of MacBooks now owns a 91 percent market share. (And this figure does not include sales of the iPad.)[1] The MacBook line isn't just different from other personal computers; it has created an emotional connection with its customers.

Level three is where everyone—regardless of the specific business or industry they're in—desires to be. Getting there is accomplished via a four-step process, which will be revealed in detail later in this book.

You can do it—*you can create distinction*—even if you or your organization is still languishing on level one.

However, you cannot do it without first attaining differentiation.

The Basics of Differentiation

Any discussion of differentiation—and how that strategy enhances profitability—must include one of the most important books ever written on the subject, Michael Porter's *Competitive Advantage: Creating and Sustaining Superior Performance.*

Porter's is one of the first books I examined as I began to study this subject. I could not help noticing that most of the ongoing studies, researched by a vastly diverse field of academics, almost always mentioned his conclusions. Let's take a very brief look at a couple of Porter's concepts and see how we can build a framework to assist you in creating distinction for yourself and your organization.

Porter believes that businesses compete using three generic strategies.

1. *Cost leadership.* The ability to produce your goods and services less expensively than your competition, which provides you with an advantage.
2. *Focus.* The concentration of your resources and efforts upon a niche or segment in the marketplace where you believe you can sustain a competitive advantage.
3. *Differentiation.* Creating a point of uniqueness that, in turn, creates viable benefits diverse from the advantages of your competitors.

When it comes to differentiation, according to Porter, there are really only three strategies an organization can employ to separate itself from the competition:

- *product* differentiation
- *price* differentiation
- *service* differentiation[2]

Let's briefly examine these three strategies and ask how you may execute these strategies at your organization.

Product Differentiation

Product differentiation means your organization is focused on designing and manufacturing a product that is clearly unique when compared to that of your competitors. This product must be perceived to be so dissimilar in and of itself that it creates the space your organization seeks in the market. This area of differentiation could be considered the "build-the-better-mousetrap" strategy. The thinking here would be stated, "If our product is significantly superior to our competition's, then we have developed a point of distinction in the marketplace."

Many better-quality products have achieved great distinction. To use an obvious example, several years ago the iPod attained superior market share because it was easier to use than other MP3 players already in circulation, it worked without hassle, and it had a coolness factor.

Therefore, it is important to honestly ask yourself and your organization this question: is the product you produce perceived by your customers and prospects as so exceptional it creates differentiation between you and your competition?

If not, then what are you going to do about it?

It seems you have three choices:

1. Start producing a differentiated product.
2. Pick another differentiation strategy.
3. Do both.

Price Differentiation

Creating price differentiation is not necessarily promoting the cheapest price.

It is *leveraging* the price you charge for your goods and services to the point that it becomes a strategic aspect of what differentiates you from the competition.

Walmart may be the first company to come to mind when we consider price differentiation. With a corporate motto of *Save Money. Live Better*, there's no doubt Walmart has determined that the prices it charges for items ranging from Tide laundry detergent to automobile batteries has become a point where it can separate itself from the competition.

And the strategy has worked pretty darn well for the company, hasn't it? The approach would seem to lend credence to researchers who advocate a *solitary* method as having the most impact in creating distinction. (Walmart is known for price leadership . . . and that's pretty much their sole source of differentiation.)

However, some automobile manufacturers—such as Bentley and Rolls-Royce—also have a price differentiation strategy. Charging a premium for their products establishes the perception of exclusivity, which, in turn, produces a special demand among the affluent prospects they target. And the value perception created, in part, by their price differentiation strategy creates a point of differentiation between Bentley and Rolls versus other luxury manufacturers such as Mercedes and Lexus.

It's pretty obvious if you are a coffee drinker that Starbucks ain't the Walmart of coffee. The price of their products, well-known and often discussed, has become the fodder for everything from university research to comedians' monologues.

However, the company's success appears to support those who are proponents of *multiple* strategies as being most effective in creating maximum differentiation. (Starbucks is known for expensive coffee . . . *and* great products, *and* wireless Internet; it is a "third place" to work and gather, and more. It has more than one point of differentiation.) Despite their more recent challenges we'll address later, Starbucks has certainly been a leader in price, service, and product selection in its industry.

Your price has to be a thoroughly designed tactic that creates differentiation to successfully employ this strategy. You can choose to be cheaper . . . or you can choose to be more expensive. However, it should be obvious that there is no differentiation in this area if your pricing is similar to that of your competitors.

The question is: is there a coherent, congruent strategy in place regarding your price, which you have leveraged to the point it becomes a factor of differentiation? Or are you just playing the game of "me too" in the marketplace?

You have three choices:

1. Lower your price to the point that it separates you from the competition.
2. Raise your price to the point that it creates significant exclusivity.
3. Or select another method of differentiation.

Service Differentiation

How do you serve your customers and prospects? Is your service different from that of your competitors? Or is the industry standard to provide a modicum of convenience, based upon your perception of your customers' desires? How do customers think of your service model (if they do), and is it in a style that provides you with a unique positioning in their minds?

Service differentiation does not necessarily imply we treat our customers better than our competition does. That is much too subjective.

I have yet to discover the organization that doesn't offer at least lip service toward the subject of customer service. All professionals and companies will tell you they deal with their customers in a service-oriented manner. (Even if too often their customers would love to tell them that they are wrong!)

Service differentiation means that we deal with customers in a manner *unique* from that of our competition. And that difference produces points to set us apart to the extent that our customers continue to choose us over our competition.

In my hometown, parents had a choice of two places to take their sons to get a haircut. I always asked Mom to take me to Sweazy's Barber Shop because Dwight Sweazy gave me a handful of candy every time I got my hair cut. The other place was friendly, and the burr haircut (or crew cut) was pretty much the same at both shops. However, for a five-year-old boy, a fistful of suckers was the service differentiation required to create sustained customer loyalty.

What would it take to create service differentiation in your category?

How could you execute a service strategy that would make customers and prospects perceive your entire efforts as differentiated?

You have two options:

1. Create a service strategy that customers find compelling enough to reward you with their business, or

2. Hope the product and/or the price will be distinctive enough you can make up for your lack of service differentiation.

"Here in the Real World . . ."

One of my favorite recording artists is Alan Jackson. He has won just about every award in the field, has sold tens of millions of CDs, and performs to sold-out arenas around the world before millions of adoring fans.

Alan Jackson's first hit was a terrific song titled, "Here in the Real World." The lyrics forlornly contrasted how romance is portrayed in the movies and on television with the everyday situations normal people experience.

Like Alan Jackson, you and I must deal with the real-life challenges of business here in the real world. This means that, in most instances, we cannot change the product mix and profile of our organizations.

Even CEOs can have their hands tied when it comes to the product line. My guess is that if you are selected as the next CEO of Apple to follow Tim Cook, you aren't going to stop making iPads. If you are the CEO of a major hotel chain, you have no chance to turn it into anything else. You have too much invested in real estate and more to execute such a dramatic twist.

And many of us cannot influence the price strategy of the goods and services we offer, either. Sure, if you are booking professional speeches and lectures, as I do, you could perhaps decide tomorrow to double your fee or to cut it in half. If you are an entrepreneur who runs a small enterprise, you may possibly have that freedom. However, the vast majority of professionals reading this book lack the ability and authority to significantly alter the price of their organization's products or services.

You already may have a firmly established position in the market based on your pricing. For example, do you remember when Walmart made a short, ill-fated venture to become a retailer of a few lines of premium-priced products? Their attempt to "out-Target" a competitor just didn't work. Walmart is a company that is just too well recognized as the go-to place for "lower prices every day."

Frankly, I was a bit embarrassed for Mercedes sales professionals who had to retail the little low-end roller skate on wheels they called the A Class a few years ago. The model was added to the Mercedes line in the United States in an attempt to sway buyers on the lower end of the price spectrum. I think the product diminished their brand and could have eroded how they were perceived in the market.

Writing in *Automotive Magazine*, Mark Gillies stated in his review the car was "a brilliant technical concept." However, he continued, "the desire to sell more cars sits, to me, uneasily, with the luster of the three-pointed star. In short, Mercedes has been devaluing one of the most respected hallmarks in the world in a Faustian swap for market share."[3]

In other words, you can be one of the most respected manufacturers in your industry, but if you have been successful at creating differentiation using the price strategy, changing your policy can wound your brand.

If you cannot impact the design of your products or control the price, then your primary point of differentiation must become service.

Nonetheless, in an interesting turn of events, the March 6, 2012, edition of *USA Today* reported Mercedes is bringing the A Class back to the United States—albeit with a model that looks a bit larger, cooler in design, and more substantial in construction and appearance. There is, however, a hidden agenda for Mercedes: this time it's not just a play to sell more cars with a product at a cheaper price; instead, it's to meet tougher environmental standards set by the U.S. government. The miles-per-gallon (mpg) rating of the small A Class will, according to the report, "help Mercedes deal with tightening federal corporate gas-mileage rules."[4] In other words, the mpg rating of the A Class will assist Mercedes to meet federally imposed standards that otherwise would be difficult for a luxury car manufacturer to attain with so many models consuming higher levels of fuel. (As of this writing, neither *USA Today* nor other publications, such as *U.S. News & World Report,* have been able to obtain a specific release date for the automobile.)

However, here is the critical factor: if you are in financial services, for example, you may have absolutely no control over pricing. Your product might be a mutual fund, for example, but the financial markets will always determine the price. You could fervently believe your fund is undervalued, yet if the market doesn't agree, you have neither the ability nor the authority to arbitrarily change the pricing.

If you cannot impact the design of your products, and if you cannot choose or control the price, then your primary point of differentiation *must* become service.

You shouldn't decry your lack of choice here, for (coincidentally or not) the strategy that can have the most significant impact on your organization and customers is the avenue most available to you. It is an approach that you can integrate into your planning and execute fairly rapidly, and it is a tactic that can create measurable long-term benefits for both customers and colleagues.

What Doesn't Work

Now that we have reviewed Michael Porter's differentiation strategies, let me suggest what will *not* differentiate you in today's world: product quality, customer service, and differentiation-strategy planning sessions.

Product Quality

You might be saying, "Wait a minute! Scott, you just reported product differentiation is one of the strategies that can develop competitive advantages. Now you are suggesting it does not?"

No, that's *not* what I'm saying. What I mean is that having a high-quality product—one manufactured with a minimum of defects, one "built to last"—is not a differentiating factor anymore.

Granted, it used to be.

There was a time years ago when building the highest-quality product would make customers stand up and take notice, and prospects would sprint to your side. No longer.

The reason is that your competitors have improved their product, just as you have improved yours. Just about every company has reasonably well-manufactured products to sell; otherwise, they would be out of business in today's marketplace. And given the rapid, vapor-like life cycle of products in many industries today, it does not take long for a competitor who may be behind to catch up with you.

"Think about Hewlett-Packard LaserJet printers. Time was, they owned the office and high-end home computer printer markets. They were fast, clean, and made documents look slick. HP printers were the best, and the company was so fast to market that its sole competition was its own next wave of printers," writes Ron Jonash, vice president and director of technology and innovation management consulting practice at Arthur D. Little, a management consulting firm based in Cambridge, Massachusetts. "Then Epson, Canon, and Lexmark caught up and joined the party, and suddenly competition in PC printers wasn't based on winning features, innovation, or service [anymore]."

He continues:

Competitors copy success. Reverse engineering a laser printer or hard drive and then gearing up production takes less time than ever. What starts out as original thinking doesn't last long. Patents and copyrights and intellectual property protection only go so far. . . . New product life-cycles for telecommunications devices and personal computer printers are measured in months.[5]

A better burger was not the answer to Alvie Kern's problem at his small-town diner. Product quality was not the issue; he had great food. It's just that a quality product wasn't enough to enable his small business to survive.

Don't get me wrong. You *must* have product quality. You are doomed without it. However, you shouldn't believe for a moment that it will—in and of itself—differentiate you or your organization in your competitive market.

Customer Service

"Okay," you're thinking, "I've got you on this one! You are clearly making the point that the vast majority of us cannot control the product or the price, so service is the only aspect left. How can you claim customer service will fail to differentiate?"

To a degree, I plead "guilty as charged." Service *is* all that remains.

However, I emphasize my point here to drive home the assertion that ordinary, run-of-the-mill customer service does nothing to make you distinct.

Consider the tourist industry in the beautiful country of New Zealand. They embarked upon a "Kiwi-friendly" effort to improve the level of customer service for visitors and then evaluated those travelers' responses to the service of which they were the supposed beneficiaries. The results showed that after their efforts to enhance their performance, "only one in three people are satisfied" with the customer service.

A survey of nearly four hundred people by service training organization KiwiHost found 67 percent of people did not get the service they wanted. KiwiHost managing director Simon Nikoloff said the key finding was service providers simply did not understand what a customer wanted.

A smile and a hello simply did not do the trick. A willingness to help, listening and understanding, and taking responsibility to help were the three outstanding gripes consumer and business customers detailed.

"We think being Kiwi-friendly is enough; the reality is that people are looking for some grunt behind that," Nikoloff said.[6]

Customer service, as traditionally defined, didn't keep the doors of Kern's Grill open either. Alvie's daughter and wife were friendly, and you didn't have to wait long to receive your order.

If you define customer service as being friendly, answering the phone quickly, moving the customer through the transaction process efficiently, and all of the other nonsense to which managers have subscribed for way too long, then you may be a nice person or organization, but you are miles away from creating the type of customer experience that will differentiate your organization.

In a later chapter, this book will outline what you need to do to create a customer experience that differentiates.

Differentiation-Strategy Planning Sessions

And that little word in the preceding paragraph—*do*—leads us to the next point that will fail to create differentiation.

I have attended and, on several occasions, I have even facilitated countless numbers of strategic planning sessions designed to examine the topic of differentiation, look at methods by which an organization can create it, and engineer processes by which it can be executed within the company.

Guess what? Most of the time these sessions don't result in any positive change.

The reason is simple: *planning* differentiation is not *doing* differentiation.

EUCG Inc. (formerly known as the Electric Utility Cost Group) reported that author and business consultant Sam Geist told attendees at the fall conference in October 2007 exactly that when he said, "Execution of a corporate strategy is more fundamental to the success of a company than the strategy itself. Without executing the strategy, nothing happens—ideas and plans disintegrate. Organizations have the propensity to strategize first, then worry about execution as a mere afterthought." Geist also noted, "This is often a setup for failure. Companies should first formulate an objective, vision, or goal and then develop the execution plan to achieve it. Execution *is* the strategy."[7]

I'm fairly certain the entire Kern family talked about what they should do to face the challenges confronting their little diner. I remember Alvie even asking my dad what steps he thought they should take. Alvie Kern pondered long and hard about what he should do, he discussed the issue with his family, and he sought advice from other small business owners in our rural community.

Then he went back to doing what he had always done.

I love the line from Sam Geist: *execution is the strategy.*

After examining the behavior of many organizations, you could infer that the strategy is to meet, not to act. Again, the reason is simple: it is easier—and perceived to be less risky—to *meet* about differentiation than it is to *execute* differentiation.

Make a difference for yourself and your organization by *creating a difference.*

Step Up!

During this time of the collapse of distinction, you must step up and create points of uniqueness for your organization and yourself. Because, just like Faber College's motto about knowledge, we know now that differentiation is good.

However, as you already know from your practical experience in today's hyper-competitive market, good enough just isn't. What do you do? Why do we perceive as superior those organizations discovering principles and practices that make them different?

In the next chapter, we'll take a look at the fundamental principle that unlocks the secret—explaining why this phenomenon has such traction in the marketplace, and providing insight on how to leverage your efforts for maximum impact.

Executive Summary

I. The three levels of business or professional differentiation are:

    A. Level One: Sameness

        1. Professionals or their organizations are fundamentally indistinguishable from their competition from the customer's point of view.

        2. Companies or professionals at this level do not have characteristics compelling enough to generate loyalty or passion regarding their products or services.

           a. Examples, from the computer industry, include Acer, Gateway, Hitachi, and Fujitsu.

    B. Level Two: Differentiation

        1. A professional or a business displays traits that set them apart from competitors.

        2. These distinguishing aspects may—or may not—provide traction in the marketplace.

        3. If you and your competition claim similar aspects as your point of differentiation, such as "customer service," the result is that there is little or no true differentiation from the customer's perspective.

           a. Examples are Sony, Dell, and HP.

    C. Level Three: Distinction

        1. You are the primary provider in your field. You are on the mind of your customer in a significant and meaningful manner.

        2. You are so uncommonly excellent that you have a clear leadership position.

        3. Organizations and individuals operating at this level are in

what author Joe Calloway categorizes as a "category of one."

a. The example is Apple.

II. According to Michael Porter's *Competitive Advantage*, there are three generic strategies for creating differentiation:

A. Product

    1. The "build a better mousetrap" strategy.

    2. Your product is significantly superior in the marketplace.

B. Price

    1. The strategy in which the price of your products or services creates space in the marketplace between you and your competition.

    2. Most initially consider this to mean low price; an example is the way Walmart created differentiation from its competitors.

    3. However, the price differentiation strategy can also mean a higher price; an example is how Rolls-Royce creates space in the market that distinguishes them from Mercedes-Benz.

C. Service

    1. Service differentiation doesn't necessarily mean we treat our customers better—it should mean that we treat them *uniquely*.

    a. "Better" is too subjective—and will be claimed as a differentiating factor by almost all.

III. In the real world, service is the primary differentiating choice.

A. Most of us cannot determine the price of our product or service.

B. Nor can we completely decide what we are building and selling.

C. However, organizationally—and individually—we can have an immediate and profound impact upon how our customers are treated.

D. If you cannot impact the design of your products, and you cannot choose or control the price, then your primary point of differentiation *must* be found in service.

IV. What will always fail to differentiate you and your organization?

   A. Product quality

      1. If your product isn't one of quality, you are probably already out of business in today's hyper-competitive market.

   B. Customer service

      1. Yes! Service makes a compelling difference.

      2. However, ordinary, run-of-the-mill, "be friendly and smile" customer service is so bland and undistinguished that it will create little to no traction for you or your organization.

   C. Differentiation-strategy planning sessions

      1. The key is to move beyond planning into execution.

      2. Planning sessions do not generate differentiation.

      3. Moving from the sessions into actual practice is where true differentiation is created.

V. Now is the time for organizations (and profound professionals) to step up and create points of uniqueness.

Action Steps, Questions, and Ideas

- My barber used candy as a service strategy for young boys to continue to get haircuts from him. What strategy keeps your customers returning for more?
- What is your differentiation strategy? List ten things that would be proof of the execution of the strategy.

FOUR

THE EBERT EFFECT

Why did Ted's Restaurant survive—even thrive—when Kern's Grill did not? What was it about these two small-town Indiana diners that caused one to fold under the pressure, to yield to the Three Destroyers of Differentiation? *What made the difference?*

After all, the two restaurants were so much alike. Sure, Kern's had fried onions on its double-decker burger, while Ted's had Thousand Island dressing, but their prices were about the same. The fried chicken platter with mashed potatoes and gravy cost the same at either place and, as I recall, tasted equally delicious.

Was it the service? Well, maybe. Both places waited on you in a timely and efficient manner. Both places put the food on the table fairly quickly.

Nevertheless, for some reason Ted's was a place where you wanted to linger, while Kern's was the diner where you most likely chose to eat and run.

In other words, while *service* was efficient in both places, the *experience* was significantly divergent at Ted's.

Certainly, McDonald's, Wendy's, Burger King, and all of the other entrants into the fast-food arena created speedy service and undoubtedly, with their resources, became superior over Kern's and Ted's in executing it. Yet it was *just different* at Ted's.

The purpose of this chapter is to reveal a powerful principle to illuminate why it is so important for any organization or professional to create differentiation.

And unlike most significant business tenets, this one was discovered through an interaction with a famous movie critic.

This concept will explain why one business can survive while another in the same industry will succumb—why one professional attains a high level of respect and recognition while another with similar qualifications remains mired in a stagnant career.

Why is "just different" so important? Because in today's marketplace, different is better. (At least customers certainly perceive it that way.)

The Ebert Effect

In one of my books, *Expand Distinction: ALL Business Is Show Business*, I describe the fortunate set of circumstances that enabled me to play the role of the villain in the highly regarded German movie *Stroszek*, and my work with the esteemed director Werner Herzog. (I play the young Wisconsin banker who repossesses the German immigrant family's mobile home.)

This marvelous event in my life later afforded me another unlikely opportunity—to become a film critic, with my commentaries syndicated to eighty television stations across the United States and around the world.

Several years ago, I attended a reception in Hollywood for movie reviewers that was sponsored by one of the major studios. There I had the occasion to meet the best in the business, Roger Ebert.

You are probably aware of Ebert's incredible body of work—from his reviews that started in the *Chicago Sun-Times* in 1967, to the Emmy-nominated *Siskel & Ebert & the Movies* that continued until Gene Siskel's passing in 1999, to *At the Movies with Ebert & Roeper*.

To my delight and surprise, the famed critic remembered the terrific review he gave my meager attempt at acting. In fact, he has often noted it is one of the "best films ever made you have never heard of," and he featured *Stroszek* in his first "Great Films" book as one of his fifty favorites. Roger asked me to sit with him and his wife, and we began a warm and fascinating conversation.

He asked me what had most surprised me about reviewing films. My response was I could not understand why so many critics offered such glowing reviews to so many foreign films that seemed, to me, to be amateurish in their script and production.

I jokingly told him I thought "many of the critics in the room would have loved *Texas Chainsaw Massacre*—if it had only been produced in Europe and shown here with subtitles."

Roger chuckled, then shocked me a bit with his response, which first came in the form of a question: "Scott, how many movies are you normally viewing in any given week?"

"One," I answered, meaning the solitary film I would be reviewing for that week's broadcast.

"Don't you see? That's your problem," he responded. "Many of the people in this profession are seeing one or two movies a *day*. Those little, offbeat, quirky, odd foreign or independent films—like the one you are in, *Stroszek*—*they* capture our attention because they are a bit different."

The wise writer continued, "When you are overwhelmed with such boring similarity, you begin to perceive that what is different is better."

The remarkable, Pulitzer Prize–winning journalist and critic taught me a great business lesson I titled the Ebert Effect: when customers—from their perspective—are inundated with indistinguishable choices, they tend to perceive a product, service, approach, or experience with a specific point of differentiation to be superior.

By the way, I continue to learn from Roger Ebert. My wife, Tammy, and I were invited to be his guests at his film festival, Ebertfest, at the University of Illinois in the summer of 2007. Roger selected *Stroszek* to be one of the main features of his event, and I was reunited with director Herzog after thirty years.

More important, we witnessed Roger's valiant battle with cancer and his extraordinary courage and commitment. He is an amazing individual with remarkable insight well beyond his considerable expertise in film.

Expand the Concept

Expand the Ebert Effect from entertainment and film to your business. How many insurance companies are there, for example? And how many differing types of policies are each of these companies offering? The number is overwhelming, both to the industry and, more important, to customers.

How many midsize, midpriced sedans sit in automobile showrooms? Could you begin to count the number of non-differentiated dealerships employing a mass of indistinguishable salespeople executing a generic sales process to sell those cars?

Consider all of the companies attempting to market everything from copiers to computers, from equipment to engineering, to your organization. Have you ever pondered the sheer number of groups out there trying to sell something to your business? Do you ever wonder why, from this myriad of marketers, you choose only a few, select vendors? (And do you wonder how you can become that "provider of choice" to the groups that you are targeting?)

On how many occasions when you were the customer have you blandly been treated like a number or an interchangeable part, whether the transaction was as a retail consumer or as part of a business-to-business sale?

The Ebert Effect noted that different is perceived to be superior. However, that difference must be *at a point that matters to the customer.*

The "different" movies—those quirky films I was discussing with Ebert—were perceived to be superior not only because they weren't exactly like the mainstream offerings; it's also because movies are critically important to a movie critic. In other words, different is perceived to be superior when that difference regards a point of importance to the customer.

It is a given in today's world that there are an overwhelming number of options available to customers. If all of the points important to the customer appear similar, then, according to the Ebert Effect, if you will display attributes that are original, clients and prospects will begin to perceive you not only as merely different but *superior* as well.

What the Ebert Effect Means to You

The Ebert Effect has many points of impact for you and your organization. Here are some of the most significant:

- It doesn't matter if you believe your product, service, or self is distinctive. The only perception that matters is the customer's.
- Although the product you sell may be incrementally enhanced over that of your competition, if you are perceived to be just another brick in a wall of sameness, your modest superiority gains you little to no traction with customers.
- If you serve your customers in a similar manner to that of your competition, you dramatically erode your product's advantages, because you have contributed to becoming indistinguishable.
- You may be so busy doing your job for your organization that you overlook or even ignore the sheer volume of similar messages your customers are receiving.

- ◆ Creating differentiation doesn't mean you have to become completely, totally unique from your competition from top to bottom. It simply means *you must create small, solid points of distinction* that are recognizable and important from the customers' perspective because *customers perceive difference as superiority*.

Why Ted's Survived

Once we understand the Ebert Effect, it becomes easier to hypothesize why Ted's remained a viable business while Kern's Grill went under.

Both were serving the same market—a small, rural town in southern Indiana. Both were serving basically the same menus. This was not a situation in which one was serving Chinese food and the other was offering Italian cuisine, making it possible to suggest the results were influenced by the culinary choices of the owner. Both had engaged proprietors and families, providing good food with good service at a reasonable price.

However, while Kern's Grill attempted, as mentioned earlier, to "out-McDonald's McDonald's," Ted's continued to be the place where customers wanted to hang around. And because there was a divergence in the experience, customers perceived a superior differentiation and responded accordingly. Customers regarded Ted's as unique and different from the drive-through, fast-food establishments. They believed Kern's was trying to keep pace with a train that had already left the station.

In other words, that little difference *was* the difference, even to the point of the life and death of the business itself.

If creating specific points of uniqueness is of primary importance, what are the specific approaches required to make it happen?

The Four Cornerstones of Distinction

Through my research and experience, I've discovered there are Four Cornerstones of Distinction. Every company and person must draw upon these qualities to develop differentiation and uniqueness in the marketplace. These cornerstones will, at first, appear to be elemental. However, the more you study them—and what is required to be successful at each—the more you will realize how spectacularly challenging it is to execute them.

When you think about it, though, this paradox may also answer an important question: why is it so rare to see true distinction? The answer is that we do not recognize or understand these cornerstones, or we fail to develop and implement the strategies necessary to execute the cornerstones—or both.

The great news, however, is that any organization or professional can change this situation instantly. As you discover the Cornerstones of Distinction, you can immediately begin to plan how you will harness their power.

The Four Cornerstones of Distinction are:

- Clarity
- Creativity
- Communication
- Customer-Experience Focus

The following chapters will explore each of these cornerstones, explain how you can develop strategies for today's hyper-competitive marketplace, and help you create distinction for yourself and your organization.

Executive Summary

I.   Why does one business succeed when the other fails?

    A. In the example of my hometown diners, one died a quick death in the face of new competition, but the other survived.

    B. Why one and not the other? What is the difference between survival and extinction?

II. The Ebert Effect

    A. Famed film critic Roger Ebert once told me that while I was seeing one movie a week, he often saw two a day—every day.

       1. He noted that often meant that movies that were different or unique in some manner would catch his attention and generate a positive response.

    B. The Ebert Effect: When customers, from their perspective, are inundated with indistinguishable choices, they perceive a product, service, approach, or experience with a specific point of differentiation to be superior.

    C. What this means to you: The Ebert Effect has many points of impact, however, perhaps the most important are:

       1. Creating differentiation does not mean you have to change everything and become completely unique from your competition.

       2. It means you must create *small, solid points* that are recognizable as different and important from the customer's perspective.

       3. From today's customer's point of view, different *is* superior.

III. The Four Cornerstones of Distinction

    A. There are four basic points that create the foundation of distinction.

B. These points appear simple; however, most organizations fail to either recognize them or to execute them.

   1. The usual result is being trapped at level one (sameness) with no plan of advancement.

C. These Four Cornerstones must be implemented—in their specific order—to create distinction for your organization and yourself.

D. The Four Cornerstones of Distinction are:

   1. Clarity

   2. Creativity

   3. Communication

   4. Customer-Experience Focus

Action Steps, Questions, and Ideas

- Keeping in mind the Ebert Effect, list five points where customers would regard you and/or your organization as being different from everything else they see in the marketplace.
- Why do you believe it is so rare to see true differentiation?
- What can you do about this phenomenon in order to distinguish yourself and your organization?

FIVE

THE FIRST CORNERSTONE:
CLARITY

There are four basic qualities every business and each professional must draw upon to develop exceptional merit in the marketplace. These are the Four Cornerstones of Distinction. The next four chapters will examine each cornerstone, and prescribe some approaches so you can build distinction for yourself and your organization.

The Four Cornerstones of Distinction are:

- Distinction is created by developing *Clarity*
- Distinction is created by developing *Creativity*
- Distinction is created by developing *Communication*
- Distinction is created by developing a *Customer-Experience Focus*

Cornerstone One: Clarity

A song that may often play in your living room is the title track of a 1978 album by the legendary rock band The Who. It's from the group's final record with drummer Keith Moon before his untimely passing from a drug overdose. This rock classic was written by The Who's guitarist, Pete Townsend, and no doubt he is still cashing big royalty checks based on its success. The song was a hit when first released; but perhaps it's better known for the many years it has played as the theme music for one of the top-rated and longest-running television shows in America,

CSI: Crime Scene Investigation on CBS. The venerable work is, of course, "Who Are You?"

To some degree this tune is playing in customers' heads when they deal with you and your organization. *What I really want to know,* they chant in their own method and manner, *is who are you?*

Why Is This So Hard to Answer?

I'm constantly asking entrepreneurial professionals and organizational managers that very question: "Who are you? How would you specifically define yourself and your company?" And guess what? Most people cannot answer the question.

By asking, "Who are you?" I do not mean your title, the company's name, or the name of the product you manufacture or the service you sell. The answer I'm seeking goes much, much deeper. I want to know what is compelling about you, what will create points of distinction about you, and what will establish a connection between us.

Here is the reason many—I suggest *most*—organizations and professionals cannot answer the question: they do not have *clarity* about who they really are.

Many organizations and professionals are so afraid of losing to the competition, they strive to become almost all things to almost all people, believing it will bring them more customers.

Play a game sometime with someone in financial services, for example. All you have to do is to innocently ask, "What do you do?"

Chances are, she will respond with a litany of products—"I insure your future with a variety of mutual funds, annuities, IRAs, and other investment instruments, as well as provide total financial solutions, including everything from mortgages to retirement planning"—or she will respond with the hot catchphrase for the current market: "I'm a wealth manager." (Some may say "wealth adviser.")

Here's the problem. In the first instance, she isn't telling you *who she is;* she is informing you about *what she sells.*

And in the second instance, she is really saying exactly the same thing—just in a more polished manner.

All you have to do with someone in the second group is to follow up with, "How much wealth does one have to invest to become the recipient of your management and advice?" She will probably view this as an opening and respond, "With a minimum of $100,000 [or $250,000 or $500,000 or whatever number she feels comfortable throwing out] I assist my clients by providing [ready for this?] a variety of mutual funds, annuities, IRAs, and other investment instruments, as well as providing total financial solutions, including everything from mortgages to retirement planning."

They're the same. It's just that the second version is slightly more sophisticated—or maybe it's merely slick.

Although this example focuses on one industry, I don't believe the situation is remarkably different in any other field.

- Abundant auto dealers want to accentuate the accoutrements of the car, believing that constitutes their business, rather than enhancing a driver's delight.

- Countless chefs center on their culinary creations instead of the real purpose of their business—developing and intensifying customer connections.

- And plentiful pharmacists pontificate on pills—because their training has centered on the medicine—rather than becoming passionate about patients.

Let me be abundantly emphatic: *who you are is not what you sell!*

Has Clarity Become Counterintuitive?

The problem for many is that this point about clarity seems counterintuitive.

"Come on," the standard response goes, "look at all those 'cliché companies'—the ones you business authors always seem to cite. Southwest is really air travel, getting people from one point to another. Starbucks is really nothing more than a glorified coffee shop."

After hearing this argument over an extended period of time, I have realized that usually this diatribe derives from people working in nondistinct organizations or from individuals representing a nondistinct company. They always want to blame someone or something else, and they make comments like these:

- "If R & D would just give us the next iPhone, everything would be fine."
- "If our frontline people were as good with customers as Southwest's, we would be doing great too."
- "If our management gave the employees health insurance and stock options like Starbucks, we would work harder for the customers."

R & D can't give you the next iPhone because it *doesn't know* what the company or its customers really want. This occurs because neither your customers nor anyone in your organization knows what the heck the company is all about.

A quote that I noted in the original version of this book—and that later gained significant notoriety because of its mention in the bestselling biography of the late Steve Jobs—is from Henry Ford, who was reported to have said that you cannot depend solely upon customers to tell you what they really want. As Jobs related the legendary Ford quotation, "If I would have asked people what they wanted, they would have answered, 'Faster horses.'"

Jobs—like Ford—however, had clarity about what he wanted his company to become and therefore about what he wanted to build and market.

You can take the same flight attendants who made Southwest unique and put them to work for your organization, and they will flounder because there isn't clarity regarding what unites their efforts.

You can have employee insurance and stock options out the wazoo, but if you aren't clear with your people about what *really* matters, you won't end up with Starbucks success. Instead, you'll have well-insured, well-optioned wandering generalities for employees.

It's Not as Easy as You Might Imagine

It's just flat-out difficult to discipline our organizations and ourselves to first discover, and then be clear about, who and what we are. My experience is that it is incredibly more challenging than most companies and professionals anticipate.

Bob Engle, CEO of CoBank, supports this point enthusiastically. CoBank, based in Denver, is one of the twenty-five largest banks in the nation and also has moved into the top ten banks in the United States in terms of commercial and indus-

> *Clarity means you are precise about who you are— and just as exact about who you are not!*

trial lending. (You'll read more about Engle and his incredible organization in my forthcoming book *Leading Distinction*.) He recently told me he was astonished to discover how remarkably difficult it is to be precise about organizational clarity—even though surveys were showing employees were scoring the company high on its corporate mission.

Part of why Engle mentioned clarity as such a difficult cornerstone is that being clear about who you are also requires that you possess clarity about who you are *not*!

It is easy to stand upon generalities and modify them so you don't lose the attention of prospective customers.

In my experience, for example, many financial advisers have stated that their practice focuses on a precise target so they may understand the specific needs of a particular group. Naturally, this approach would enable the advisors to provide a special and distinct service. But then people who fail to fit the target profile come along and want to invest—and the advisers take their business anyway.

When I ask them why they moved away from the clarity that would provide distinction, these sophisticated professionals have said in all seriousness, "But what if they win the lottery and I had turned them away?" Good grief! If that has become the accepted standard, these advisers should start prospecting at convenience stores, because that's where most winning tickets are sold.

People always respond to this by asking me if this "clarity stuff" means an organization or professional should turn away customers.

The answer is *yes!*

As you discover the other Cornerstones of Distinction, you will come to understand that truly differentiated organizations *never* try to attract everyone. Through their clarity, they take themselves out of the running for the business of some potential customers.

Take a look at what Starbucks is doing right now. Just a few years ago, the Starbucks brand began having trouble. (So much difficulty, they brought back their legendary CEO Howard Schultz, who announced, "Over the years we kind of lost our way.")

Schultz's company had attempted, in my opinion, to become too many things to too many people. Serving breakfast sandwiches, for example, doesn't strike me as really what Starbucks is supposed to be about. People wanting a hot breakfast sandwich should not have become a target customer for Starbucks. Once the company lost the "coffee" focus, customers had to wonder: Where will it end? What's next—burgers for lunch?

No! If you want a burger, my suggestion is that you go to Wendy's. And if a gourmet coffee drink like a latte or cappuccino is what you seek at midday, then Wendy's *should fire you* from its target lunch prospects.

To regain its distinctiveness in the market, Starbucks has made some terrific decisions. As Janet Adamy reported in the *Wall Street Journal* on February 27, 2008, Starbucks closed nearly every store in the entire chain—7,100 locations—for three hours to give managers the opportunity to tell their baristas (their employees) who Starbucks *really* is.

At a Starbucks in downtown Chicago, about a dozen workers slurped samples of coffee and discussed how it smelled. They explained to each other how they conversed with their regular customers while managers gave them pointers on how to improve the interaction. Some of the Chicago baristas told managers they sometimes feel too rushed to give customers the best service and that they have difficulty remembering regular customers' names.

Starbucks leadership realized they had wandered from their distinctive clarity and decided what they must return to their stores—an experience similar to what they had provided for their customers in the early days of their remarkable success. They had to make it clear to every employee what Starbucks stood for in the marketplace. "It should be a wow factor," said Andrew Alfano, regional vice president for the Starbucks Midwest region.[1]

The results since this point was initially written in 2008. By refocusing on clarity—and executing on the additional cornerstones to follow—as of January 2012, Starbucks stock was up 140 percent.

Great insight into the situation is provided by a post by Amy Chulik on the website CareerBuilder.com:

Over time, the company had been expanding the brand beyond its core into various media like music, books, and film. Amidst battle cries of "More growth!" the team had lost sight of what the Starbucks experience was really all about. Starbucks, [Schultz] pointed out in his book, has always been about so much more than coffee.

"But without great coffee," he wrote, "we have no reason to exist."[2]

What is *your* "reason to exist"? And, like Howard Schultz, would you have the guts to shut down your business—*system-wide*—for three hours to make certain there is clarity throughout your organization about who you really are, and what it means to customers?

The Example of a Presidential Campaign

Major national campaigns that candidates undertake for political office are, in fact, big businesses seeking to convert prospects (called "constituents") into customers ("voters"). Perhaps no political operation in the history of our nation overcame greater odds or was executed as flawlessly as the 2008 presidential campaign of Barack Obama.

It's important to note that an appreciation of the manner in which President Obama organized and executed his 2008 campaign is not intended to be an endorsement (or rejection) of his policies since his assuming the highest office in the land. Any professional or company should possess an open mind toward learning from one of the best-managed organizations in recent memory, regardless of your political persuasion.

When Obama originally announced his campaign from the steps of the Illinois Old State Capitol—the same spot where Abraham Lincoln gave his "house divided" speech in 1858—he was perceived to be just one of the many challengers to the presumptive nominee of the Democratic Party, former First Lady (later Secretary of State) Hillary Rodham Clinton.

However, Obama understood how the Ebert Effect would work to his benefit. Just by being different from the candidates who had been around before—Mrs. Clinton, John Edwards (whose life has certainly changed since this campaign because of a messy personal scandal), Joe Biden (who became Obama's vice president), and Chris Dodd (now the CEO of the Motion Picture Association of America)—there was a percentage of the electorate that would perceive him as a superior choice from the beginning.

Most important, though, for our discussion is an examination of the precise manner in which Barack Obama's first candidacy for the office was differentiated from those of his competitors—first in the Democratic primaries, and then in the general election versus John McCain—because it displays a comprehensive implementation of the Four Cornerstones of Distinction.

Barack Obama understood and implemented the first cornerstone: clarity. As David Brody, senior national correspondent for CBN (Christian Broadcasting Network) News, reported the night of the historic election, "There are several reasons why Barack Obama won the 2008 presidential election. But let me tell you in one simple sentence why he triumphed: Barack Obama will become the next President of the United States because he defined himself early with a *clear* message [emphasis added]."[3]

While other candidates were running all over Iowa and New Hampshire offering their viewpoints on Iraq, the economy, the Bush administration, and assorted other topics, Barack Obama's message was simple, profound, and clear: he was the candidate of hope and change.

When he expressed his positions on the issues other candidates were tackling, Obama almost always presented his points as seen through the prism of "hope and change." Looking back from the perspective of several years, it's hard now to remember a short, powerful phrase that describes any other candidate's efforts. Obama's clearness emphasized the power of his message—and accelerated his rise to the top.

When the Democratic primaries were narrowed down to two major candidates from the eight that began the process, Hillary Clinton's higher name recognition was muted by the clarity of Barack Obama's message.

Later in 2008, when John McCain had secured his party's nomination, it was too late for him to position himself as a leader for change—something that, perhaps, would have enabled him to distance himself from the unpopular Bush administration. Barack Obama clearly owned the "change" message, and it was one voters plainly desired to hear.

For the 2012 campaign, now-President Obama discovered he couldn't use his same "Hope and Change" clarity statement for a second race for the same office. Perhaps it is not impossible—but it is certainly very challenging—for any incumbent to be the candidate for "change." Therefore, "Forward" meant a continuation of the policies Obama viewed as generating hope and change. Frankly, it's not the most compelling statement of clarity—however, what was the opponent's? It often seemed the Mitt Romney campaign's primary point was: "He's Not Obama." We know from the results of the 2012 election that this wasn't a message with enough clarity to carry a majority of the electorate.

You must have clarity to create distinction—and you are required to execute upon your clarity to maintain distinction. This critical aspect will be discussed in the final chapter of this book.

"We Are That Too"

As I was writing the initial version of this book, I was involved in a series of consulting assignments with multimillion-dollar producers affiliated with the largest financial service brokerage in the country. As a result of the research developed by my good friend Dr. Rick Jensen of the Performance Center, located at PGA National Resort in Parkland, Florida, we know the highest performing financial advisers have developed highly specialized practices and extraordinary clarity regarding their points of distinction in the marketplace.

In eight separate meetings in a single day, I asked leading professionals in the field, "What differentiates your practice from those of other financial advisers?" Six times I received the response, "We provide great client service." Twice, the answer was, "I don't know."

Consider that for a moment: these are *successful* professionals! Granted, they may not be the absolute best of the best, but they certainly aren't failures, either. Yet somehow they have missed the point that if they want to achieve higher levels of success and profitability, the most important step they can take is to make their practice differentiated from the scores of others in the same business.

Do they really think "great client service" is a differentiator? Does that mean that others in their industry are indicating they provide "pretty awful client service" to their investors? I doubt it.

I then asked them to describe their best client or most likely prospect. Some said, "surgeons." Others responded with "corporate executives" or professionals in other positions of affluence.

However, when I asked the advisers who stated the targets and specialty of their practice to be "surgeons" if they would also accept as a client a corporate CEO who wanted to invest $250,000, all of them responded, "Well, we are that *too*!"

You cannot differentiate
a generic.

The problem is, you cannot be "that *too!*" and create distinction in your field.

The top financial advisers I have worked with are highly specialized. For example, they work *exclusively* with surgeons. Rick Jensen knows one professional who works only with PGA golfers—and another who works only with people involved in the sport of polo.

If you have a pool of cash to invest but are not a part of the polo scene, this particular adviser will refer you to someone else. (And, according to Dr. Jensen, he *has!*) By the way, Rick Jensen also reports that by turning away the business that is not a good fit, they have become among the most profitable of all professionals in their industry.

If I focus on surgeons, for example, as my clearly defined client base, I can learn their schedules, participate in their charitable activities, understand their unique professional challenges, educate myself in some of their specialized terminology, host client events that appeal to their specific needs, plan my work hours to fit the times that are easiest to contact them and be contacted by them, and much more.

However, this also answers the question of why so few in any (and every) profession are able to attain significant distinction.

Can you begin to imagine how difficult it is to learn all of this and more about a specific customer base? Therefore, we usually end up—organizationally and individually—knowing our *products* but not our *customers*. We're often a mile wide and an inch deep when it comes to knowing what would really make a difference for the very people we seek to serve. Or we try to serve so many that we end up truly engaging very few.

The truth is you don't have enough time or energy to create highly distinctive customer experiences for a widely varied assembly of wildly diverse customers.

On the other hand, you might say that Walmart sells "everything to everybody"—but that would not be accurate.

What if you want a tuxedo? What about a designer gown? You cannot find them at Walmart. Marketing low prices every day on mass-market consumer items is clearly what Walmart is all about. There is a sizable amount of clarity regarding who the company is, even though it handles thousands of items.

Here's part of the reason clarity is so vital: you cannot differentiate a generic.

Professionals simply cannot provide the kind of clarity and intense differentiation required for ultimate success if their focus is diluted. In the field of medicine, for example, we take for granted that the specialist is more highly compensated than the general practitioner. Usually, specialists are not the ones giving referrals to the GPs; it's the other way around. Why would we presume other industries would have a different set of rules?

How Do You Become Clear?

If you are not clear, you have to get there. One of the best exercises I've developed for clarity stems from an approach I related in my first business book, *Expand Distinction: ALL Business Is Show Business*. It's called the "high concept" principle.

This isn't original to me. High concept is a principle Hollywood and the entertainment industry have long understood as vital for creating and marketing their products.

For example, the concept or plot of a movie would tell you what that movie is all about. However, Hollywood recognized that people today have neither the time nor the inclination to listen to a long, involved concept or plot.

The high concept is a *short, powerful phrase* that grabs the attention and engages the involvement of your audience.

I can say, "Bomb on a bus," and you think of the movie *Speed*. (Which is pretty remarkable when you consider the film was made in 1994 . . . and it took you just four minutes short of two hours to watch . . . and two decades later I can state just four words and you know what film I am referring to!) To continue the point, "Shark attack!" still elicits the response of *Jaws*. "Teenager bitten by spider develops superpowers," is, of course, *Spiderman*.

For the entertainment industry, the potential audience for whom they want to "grab attention and engage involvement" is you and me. For your business, the audience is obviously your customers and prospects.

One new development has occurred since I first wrote about this approach years ago. Now Hollywood occasionally makes the title of the movie the *same* as the high concept.

Not long ago, there was a Samuel L. Jackson movie called *Snakes on a Plane*. (You don't really have to wonder what that movie is about, do you? If you were sitting in the theater and were astonished to see snakes on the plane, you were not paying attention as you walked past the ticket seller and the movie posters.) No doubt, the high concept—which became the title—presented extraordinary clarity about the film.

> *The high concept is a short, powerful phrase that engages your audience.*

Visionary companies in today's entertainment-oriented times understand that this principle works not just for movies but for their organizations as well. Here's an example: "Your pizza in thirty minutes!"

What company did you think of? Of course, *Domino's*!

With all due respect, few customers have ever picked up the phone to call Domino's because it is the all-time, best-tasting pizza the customer has ever consumed. Customers call Domino's because the company provides a darn good pizza that is delivered rapidly. That's a factor of distinction. And it is marketable, repeatable, recognizable, and referable for a simple reason: it is clear. Domino's knows who it is.

Even as their current commercials point to their renewed efforts emphasizing product quality—to make certain we know Domino's makes really, really good pizza as well as offering fast delivery—the company is not attempting to be a gourmet pizza establishment and imitate a restaurant like Wolfgang Puck's Spago in Beverly Hills.

Instead, the people at Domino's are clear that their point of distinction is they deliver a really good pizza to you, very rapidly.

It's interesting, too, that a competitor of Domino's in the same market—Papa John's—emphasizes their clarity regarding their point of differentiation: "Better Ingredients, Better Pizza." In other words, even though Papa John's delivers at many locations, the company has put its respective flag in the ground of "great pizza," while a competitor like Domino's is clear that their point is "fast delivery." It allows both organizations to successfully create distinction—even as they compete in the same industry.

(As an aside, my late wife, Sheri, was often "Papa" John Schnatter's babysitter. Even when he began his company in southern Indiana with his first store, he was proud of the quality of his product.)

When the iPod was released, Apple did not describe it as an MP3 player or any of the other terms that competitors in the category of portable music players were using at the time. Instead, as related by Adam Lashinsky, senior editor-at-large for *Fortune* in an address to students at Stanford on May 23, 2012, Apple simply used the powerful high-concept slogan "1,000 songs in your pocket."

This establishes an important aspect of clarity: customers don't care about *how* you do it; they care that you *can* do it in a way that benefits them.

Frankly, when I stop to think about it, I'm fairly certain it is difficult to make a pizza and get it to my doorstep as rapidly and deliciously as Domino's makes it happen. However, in the final analysis, I really don't care how they do it. I just want my pizza delivered hot and on time! I know the technology of the first iPod I purchased was innovative; however, that's not what matters. I just want "1,000 songs" in *my* pocket!

As you develop your high concept, make certain the essence of the statement is what your product or service or organization delivers for the customers (external or internal) you seek to retain and attract.

The Personal High Concept

Following my presentation to a group of successful financial consultants, one of the attendees asked me to review the high-concept statement he had prepared. It was this: "I will help secure your financial future."

My response to his effort was to smile and say, "Boring!" His high concept failed to be interesting because every financial consultant from the newest life insurance salesperson to a very senior wealth manager could make an identical statement. His high concept had no degree of uniqueness.

As we discussed the importance of distinction, he related to me that he was, in fact, now beginning his second career. In his first he was an air force fighter pilot. I told him to use that unique personal and professional aspect in his high-concept statement; it would make him distinctive.

His individual high concept is now this: "I fly clients through today's financial turbulence!" My response to that? "Exciting!" Wouldn't you want to know more?

Creating Your High Concept

Consider three fundamental questions as you develop your high concept statement:

1. What makes your business (or you) different from your competition?
2. What makes you better than your competition?
3. What makes you and your organization unique?

If you cannot answer these questions, neither can your customers or employees.

High Concept and the USP

Many "old style" sales training programs discussed a point they titled the *unique selling proposition* (USP). Every salesperson in the course was instructed to clearly classify what made their sales proposal inimitable from the customer's perspective.

In the old days, the USP usually centered on a specific feature or fact about the *product*. In today's world, the product approach has a diminished degree of value because customers tend to focus much less on facts about products and much more on their customer experience and on how they *feel* about dealing with you.

Your high concept, like the USP, should be a concise statement. However, it does not need to be limited to a single specific product or service advantage.

Continue to develop your high concept by asking your colleagues and yourself these questions:

- What are the defining values of our organization?
- Are they outlined in our mission statement?
- Could they form the basis of our high-concept statement?

Next, brainstorm a high concept with your colleagues. Then, ask this question: are these the same points our *customers* would make about us? If they are, you are on your way.

Finally, here's a role-playing exercise. After your brainstorming session, ask your colleagues: how are the responses we've given *different* from those our competition would provide?

If they're not different, neither your high concept nor your organization is truly unique.

Not Just for the Entire Organization

The idea of a high concept is not limited to a broad application focusing on the total organization.

As I've suggested, individuals also need a high concept as a starting point on the road to the clarity necessary to build distinction. In addition, if you are seeking to create distinction within your company—for your department, for example—the high concept is a terrific place to begin.

Several years ago, I was the keynote speaker for the annual meeting of the American Payroll Association, which is led by its dynamic and highly creative CEO, Dan Maddux.

The challenge I addressed for the group was that most employees in their departments would probably define their jobs as merely "cutting payroll checks." Let's face it; few people become motivated and excited about going to the office and creating distinction by simply "cutting checks." Now, several of the payroll departments of the organizations in attendance have signs on the walls of their offices with their new, distinctive high concept: "We deposit the money that funds the dreams of thousands of families—including our own!" They're not merely cutting checks; they're *funding dreams!*

There's no doubt that many will read about determining the high concept and consider the exercise to be futile in today's volatile economy. They may feel it is corny and childish, providing platitudes that accomplish little in the way of profitability and sales.

I obviously disagree. I believe the high concept is the *starting point in the development of distinction.*

You Cannot Differentiate What You Cannot Define

Back in the days when it was still called by its full name, Federal Express, all FedEx employees clearly understood what the company was about: getting a package from one customer to another absolutely, positively overnight.

If an employee saw a misplaced package sitting on the dock, would he whimsically state, "Oh, well. We'll get it there tomorrow. Better late than never"? Of course not! He would move heaven and earth to get the package where it was supposed to go—and arriving at the time it was supposed to be there—because it was abundantly clear who the organization was. The company delivered absolutely, positively overnight.

Has the FedEx of today altered itself a bit? Certainly! Through acquisition and growth, the company offers more delivery options in shipping, logistics management, and even printing and copying to its millions of customers. Correspondingly, note a change in the high concept FedEx later promoted: "Why fool around with anybody else?" In other words, the time frame or transportation may now be variable; however, the dependability is absolutely not.

Sometimes You Clearly Have to Change

In the real world, we sometimes have to alter our business path.

When I'm emphasizing clarity, I'm not suggesting that along the way you can make absolutely zero changes whatsoever to the strategies you develop as an outgrowth of this approach.

For example, after Apple Computer had success with the iPod line, it shortened its name to become Apple, Inc. Nothing wrong with that—especially when you are clear and precise that your focus is creating the most compelling, gotta own, high-tech devices on the planet.

But say you find that times have dramatically changed. First, you understand and appreciate that there has been clarity about what you've *been*. Now you need to establish clarity about what you *will become*.

An extraordinary example of this approach is found at an exceptional university.

Success in Higher Education

Earlier I mentioned my very close friend of many years Dr. Nido Qubein, now president of High Point University. A member of the executive committee and board of directors of financial giant BB&T and the chairman of the board of Great Harvest Bread Company, Qubein was already a multimillionaire businessman, author, and speaker when he decided to make a significant difference for his alma mater and accepted the offer to become the university's leader.

One of the first aspects Qubein introduced to the institution was the initiation of an effort to become extraordinarily precise about its points of differentiation, in order to begin to create clarity and distinction.

Consider for a moment HPU's competition for students: within just a few miles are such nationally renowned institutions of higher learning as Duke University, the University of North Carolina (UNC), and Wake Forest. Just a little farther down the road is North Carolina State University. How could a small college like HPU compete against UNC and the others?

First, upon assuming the duties of the presidency, Qubein created a high concept for his university. It's a brilliant one that both students and parents love:

"At High Point University, every student receives an extraordinary education in an inspiring environment with caring people."

Who would not want to be a part of that?

However, it's easy to overlook the depth of the statement, as well. It requires the university to deliver on this promise to every student, not just those receiving scholarships or studying at an honors level.

The education has to be extraordinary—not simply the certification of a degree—and that's a pretty tall order when you consider the competitive atmosphere for the best students available.

And although many of us may remember inspiring times during our college years, I doubt a significant portion of us would state that our institution of higher learning was also committed to creating an "inspiring environment." Yet High Point University makes that pledge to its prospective students as well as those currently enrolled.

Finally, HPU vows to students and their parents that the faculty and staff consist of "caring people." I imagine your experience in college was similar to mine. Some exceptional professors routinely displayed intense concern for their students, while others really didn't care whether their students passed or failed. At High Point University, caring people create differentiation.

High Point University will be an example we will visit again, and we will examine its results. Remember, clarity is only the *first* cornerstone. Dr. Qubein and HPU will have to put several more stones in place to truly differentiate their institution and achieve distinction; however, this is a vitally important process to begin to execute.

You cannot differentiate what you cannot define. }

Remember, *you cannot differentiate what you cannot define.* Therefore, your goal is to be as precise as possible about who you are and what your organization is and what it is not. Be ready to fire prospects and customers who fail to fit your format.

Clarity is essential because those same customers asking, "Who are you?" will not present you with multiple opportunities to define yourself. After dealing with so many nondistinct organizations and professionals, they are vowing they "won't get fooled again."

However, you can be clear about who and what you are—and clearly be *boring*! If you cannot engage your colleagues, customers, and prospects, how can you expect them to perceive that you have created distinction?

That's why it is critical to move to the second Cornerstone of Distinction: creativity!

Executive Summary

I. The First Cornerstone: Distinction is created by developing *clarity*.

    A. A question that most organizations and professionals cannot answer precisely is: *Who are you?*

    B. Most cannot specifically define themselves or their organization.

        1. The answer is not the company name, product name, or a recitation of the mission statement.

        2. It goes much deeper than that: What is compelling? What will create a point of differentiation—and connect us to our customer?

    C. Many organizations and professionals are so afraid of losing to their competitors that they strive to become "all things to almost all people."

        1. They believe it gives them more opportunity to attract customers.

        2. Instead, it dilutes their differentiation, making them indistinguishable in the marketplace.

    D. Excuses must stop!

        1. Even if your organization has the products of Apple, the people of Southwest, and the benefit packages of Starbucks, it won't make a meaningful difference if you fail to create clarity about what makes you distinctive in the market.

II. It's not as easy as it seems!

    A. Because the cornerstone of clarity means that you are precise about what you are, it also means you are exact about what you are not.

    B. It is difficult for any organization or professional to "fire" a customer. Yet attempting to be "all things to almost all people" is a major factor in diluting distinction.

1. Starbucks admitted it "kind of lost its way" when it added everything from breakfast sandwiches to music to the product line. Be clear about what you are—and focus on your distinction.

2. If you, like the financial professionals cited in the text, cannot define precisely who and what you are, you are inviting the customers with the highest potential to go elsewhere.

   a. The prospects with the most promise are also the ones who seek specialists for their providers.

   b. Sending a message that "well, we are that, *too*," means that you will remain a "general practitioner" in a world that more highly rewards "specialists."

C. The truth is that you have neither the time nor the energy to create highly distinctive customer experiences for a widely varied assembly of wildly diverse customers.

   1. Not even Walmart sells everything to everybody!

III. The process of creating clarity

A. "High concept" principle

   1. "Shark attack" makes you think of the movie *Jaws*. "Bomb on a bus" makes you think of the movie *Speed*. These are high concepts from popular movies—and examples of the high-concept principle created by Hollywood.

   2. It works in corporate America, as well: "Your pizza in thirty minutes" makes you think of Domino's.

B. Individual professionals also should create high-concept statements.

IV. Creating your high concept

A. Consider these fundamental questions:

   1. What makes your business (or you) different . . . better . . . unique . . . in comparison to your competition?

    2. If you cannot answer these questions, neither can your employees or customers!

  B. Brainstorm with your colleagues

    1. What are the defining values of our organization?

    2. What is espoused in our mission statement?

    3. How could these points form the basis of a high-concept statement?

    4. How are they different from the aspects our competitors might use in their statements?

  C. Create a short, powerful "grabbing" statement that interests and involves your audience of customers, colleagues, and prospects.

V. High concepts are not just for the entire organization—every department within the organization requires one as well.

  A. "We deposit the money that funds the dreams of thousands of families, including our own" (from the payroll department of a major corporation).

VI. Sometimes you have to change

  A. At times, organizations go through changes—or wish to initiate change—and therefore must alter their high concept.

    1. Apple Computer, Inc., became just Apple, Inc., with the success of the iPod.

VII. Clarity is the starting point

  A. At High Point University, the new president, Dr. Nido Qubein, created a high-concept statement as the starting point for the enhancements he wanted to create for the institution.

  B. "At High Point University, every student receives an extraordinary education in an inspiring environment with caring people."

    1. As we progress, we will observe how the actions of the institution were generated from the clarity the new leader created.

VIII.   "You cannot differentiate what you cannot define."

    A. Start now. If you do not begin the process, it cannot create the results you desire.

Action Steps, Questions, and Ideas

- Who are you and your organization? How would you specifically define yourself to your customers? What are you all about? What will establish a connection with customers that is different from that of your competition? Please write down your answers, and do not list what you sell.

- If I asked one of your customers to describe you or your organization, what would he say? Would he be clear about who and what you are?

- How would you describe your target customers? What are they looking for? Who are they?

- When you describe yourself or your organization to customers—particularly if you relate your high concept to them—how is it different from the language that your competition would use?

SIX

THE SECOND CORNERSTONE:

CREATIVITY

Certainly you can possess abundant clarity about your organization and yourself—and bore your customers to death!

Obviously, while it is a great first step to be precise about what you are—and what you are not—it isn't the solitary requirement for creating distinction. This chapter will examine the importance of the cornerstone of creativity. You'll learn:

- Why creativity must follow clarity in building distinction
- A three-step strategy for inspiring the innovation to advance you beyond your competition
- And, perhaps kindling a bit of controversy, this chapter will reveal why if you decide to forgo creativity to merely follow well-publicized "best practices"—including ones from a mega-bestselling business book—it may not produce the results you desire.

In *Corporate Creativity*, a leading book on the topic of creativity and business, authors Alan G. Robinson and Sam Stern make the point that "creativity is essential to the workplace." (Who would argue with that?) Nevertheless, "in most companies, potential creativity far exceeds creative performance."[1]

But is that assertion really surprising? Consider our previous examples of non-differentiated professionals and organizations. Innovations are often focused on incremental improvements that do not require exceptional originality. And since many of us aren't really clear on who we are—or even whom we really seek to serve—the bar for inventiveness and imagination is set pretty low.

Author Bruce Airo addresses this in the magazine *Supervision*:

Creativity probably got a bad rap from many sources along the way. From our teachers on into adulthood, much of our influence has been to conform. Do the safe thing. Don't take risks. Do what everyone else is doing. We can view our lives as one long effort to toe the line. What a joy then when we can see another side. It's like a precious gift. Allowing and even promoting creativity is like that. Won't everything fall apart if everyone is going willy-nilly around doing their own independent thing? No, it doesn't mean that.[2]

Airo concludes, "Creativity is not equivalent to anarchy. It is different in an essential way. Anarchy is an absence of any structure. Creativity is an instinct to produce."[3]

Airo's article makes an important point. Often when I speak to organizations and managers about the importance of creativity within the process of developing differentiation, they act as if I am inviting chaos. I love the manner in which Airo defines the difference between these characteristics. He really explains why creativity is the second Cornerstone of Distinction.

Creativity Is Second

Visualize, if you will, a writer sitting down at her laptop with the "instinct to produce" and beginning to type. Could you even imagine she would not know what the precise medium was going to be of the creative product she was producing?

Obviously, the answer is no. In other words, even when the most innovative artists in the world begin to develop from the fruits of their imagination, they are already crystal clear about the specific format for which they are creating. Clarity about the work comes before creativity within the work.

An author doesn't just start creating without already knowing whether she is developing a novel, a screenplay, a song, or a poem. And no matter how wildly original her imagination, the artist still respects, at least to some degree, the restrictions of the format she has selected. As trite and obvious as it sounds, songs require notes, paintings usually are made using brushes and canvas, and novels depend upon words.

Yet herein lies much of the difficulty I've observed when organizations encourage their colleagues to "think outside the box." They somehow believe that creativity is stimulated exclusive of restrictions. But, as we see here, even the most creative artists understand that there are inherent limitations to any form. This is why developing creativity is the second Cornerstone of Distinction.

Creativity without clarity is devoid of distinction.

"But I'm Not Creative!"

Before we spend too much time on the restrictions, let's examine how you can become more creative.

Countless authors offer ideas on how a professional or an organization can become more creative. Amazon lists nearly 9,000 books on creativity and business, and almost 200,000 on creativity alone; it would seem from all the discussion and authors' positions that creativity is a difficult science—but that's not so. The codirector of Harvard University's Project Zero study of cognitive skills in the sciences and humanities, David N. Perkins, has said creativity "has little to do with intelligence, talent, or expertise. These may provide the raw horsepower for creative endeavors, but not the steering."[4]

In other words, *everyone* can do it.

Here are three ideas for stimulating and steering creativity that we will employ within the confines of the clarity we have already determined.

Creative Idea #1: Believe You Are Creative

One of my favorite sayings comes from the book *A Whack on the Side of the Head* by Roger von Oech. He states that the key to being creative is simply believing that you are. That's it!

So when someone protests, "But I'm not creative," the process immediately shuts down. The moment you tell yourself you are devoid of creativity, you build a dam across the free flow of ideas. However, people who believe that they are creative can easily begin to generate ideas and concepts.

Creative Idea #2: Expose Yourself to Stimulus

Another question you must ask yourself is, "Am I being exposed to stimulus that will generate creativity?"

My good friend Randy Gage is a remarkable person who has risen from being a high school dropout to now earning acclaim as the "Millionaire Messiah" because his strategies have assisted so many of his clients in creating wealth. Randy has been quoted as saying:

Creative people generally are self-motivated, independent, delighted by novelty, risk takers, tolerant of ambiguity, deeply involved in their work, avid readers, and world travelers. These characteristics provide creative people with a very rich diet of stimulation, variety, and situations. They see the same thing handled in many different ways, so it opens up the mind to problem solving, lateral thinking, and innovation.[5]

The person or organization desiring to enhance creativity must ask if there is—*in his or her immediate environment*—the systematic exposure to stimuli, such as Randy notes, that can nurture the essential spirit necessary to possess an open and productive mind. Ask yourself right now, "Have I put myself on 'a very rich diet of stimulation'?" If not, what action will you take to do so?

Creative Idea #3: Understand That Creativity Is Synergistic

If there is one word in the business vernacular I feel has been overused, it is "synergy," which describes a greater-than-the-sum outcome resulting from the combination of two or more forces. We often lump people or departments together with no apparent motive other than the rationalization or hope that the move will create synergy.

Organizations acquire a competitor and promise Wall Street the merger will produce greater profits because of the new synergies. Many times, investors have been highly disappointed in the results.

Nevertheless, if there is one place that this concept actually works, it is in the area of creativity.

For some mystical reason, creativity is extraordinarily difficult in a vacuum. Ideas improve when shared with others. As George Endres, former senior vice president for distribution of mutual funds for global financial giant Old Mutual, often reminds his colleagues, "None of us is as smart as all of us."

A brief article in *R&D* magazine informs us "Collaborative technologies are vital to continual innovation. Sharing knowledge across a research group, organization, or partnership sparks the breakthrough thinking necessary for the creation of new products and new ways of doing business."[6]

I can certainly state from personal experience that the concepts in this book and in my previous works have greatly benefited from sharing and discussing (sometimes to the point of arguing) them with friends who have alternative viewpoints. And, most likely, the fact that my friends and colleagues are willing to bicker and vibrantly discuss the issues is the most important point as we consider creativity.

A January 30, 2012, article for *The New Yorker* titled "Groupthink: The Brainstorming Myth" reveals how the typical approach of "brainstorming," pioneered in the late 1940s by Alex Osborn and advertising agency B.B.D.O., doesn't produce the best results.

The problem with the standard procedure of brainstorming, according to the article and research dating back to a Yale study in the 1950s, is instead of the brainstorming process producing greater results, it's people working alone initially, *then* sharing and discussing their results with others, that characteristically provided results with significantly higher impact.

The article suggests, "The fatal misconception behind brainstorming is that there is a particular script we should all follow in group interactions." It continues, "It's the human friction that creates the sparks." [7] (Creativity does have its ethical limits. Several months after this article appeared, its author Jonah Lehrer resigned his position at *The New Yorker* after admitting he had fabricated quotes, then lying about sources when confronted. While controversial, Lehrer's quotes and observations used here have not been among those of disputed accuracy.)

A word of caution, however: be careful about who you choose to invite to become a part of your creativity group. We all know those people who brighten a room when they leave it! We are looking for those willing to debate and challenge, but not those who respond negatively simply in order to assert a degree of influence or power. Don't bring creativity killers into your circle of synergy.

Stimulating Productive Creativity

If you are going to inspire productive creativity—the kind that can stimulate strategies that will have immediate positive impact on you and your organization—here are the three action steps you should take.

Step One: Drive It Down

Your first step is to rely upon your clarity to break down all customer interaction into the smallest units or steps possible.

Ask yourself this question: what is every point of contact a customer has with me or my organization? Make an extremely detailed list.

During the Q&A session at a recent program in Portland, Oregon, one member of the audience remarked that her company had "kind of forgotten that our product has to be installed." When I asked her for more insight into her problem, she continued, "We sell business communication systems that include everything from the actual telephone handsets to the service for telephone, wireless, Internet, and television. We have many wonderful advantages our sales team works hard to communicate. Yet we never included the installers in this process. Therefore, we are getting frequent complaints our technicians aren't creating positive experiences for our customers."

She captured the essence of why it is so important to keep "driving it down" (Step One). Although many organizations are highly aware of the quality of communication between the salesperson and the customer, not nearly as many consider the impact of other representatives on the customer experience.

Now the important question: what happens when customers are in contact with you?

It's time to be very specific about the process. If you are like most organizations—or professionals—you aren't finding too much in the way of differentiation.

For example, when a customer rents a car, it seems these are the twelve basic points and stages of contact:

1. Call the agency (or travel agent) and make a reservation, or use the website of the agency or travel company to secure a reservation.

2. Travel to the agency location by its bus (at the airport) or by other arranged transportation (for local locations).

3. Enter the agency and proceed to the counter.

4. Process paperwork and provide payment for the reservation.

5. Obtain driving directions.

6. Proceed to the rental car.

7. Exit the lot through security.

8. Drive the rental car for the period outlined in the contract with the agency.

9. Return the car to the agency location.

10. Determine the final cost of the rental based upon the contract agreement and the fuel level when the car is returned.

11. Complete car check-in.

12. Depart agency.

The next step should be to develop a similar list of the points of customer contact for your industry in general and your organization in particular.

It's important that you drive this down to the most precise aspects possible. Every point of contact with your customer provides an opportunity for distinction.

Consider the automobile manufacturer and dealer network for a moment. It takes years to engineer a new model of automobile. And as we have seen with the dramatic rise in the cost of gasoline, sometimes highly popular models—like SUVs—can fall out of favor rapidly.

Dealers, however, could engage in new approaches to immediately distinguish themselves from the competition with creative improvements throughout the dealership. For example, here are some ideas:

* Greet each prospective customer with a concierge.
* Offer no-haggle pricing.
* Follow up initial contact with telephone calls.
* Maintain ongoing contact between sales consultants and customers.
* Stage wine-tasting events in the showroom with new luxury car models.
* Provide special driving programs associated with local racing events—perhaps even with NASCAR or IndyCar drivers—for sports car enthusiasts.
* Create distinctly different advertising.

All these—and more—are ways to begin to create distinction.

Yes, I realize some dealers are already doing some of these steps and that all of this sounds fairly obvious, so I would suggest the most important question one in the automotive business must ask is, "Why aren't *more* dealers already doing these things?"

It doesn't stop there, however. If I am an employee of the dealership, I must find creative strategies and techniques that will differentiate me from everyone else. The top salespeople get the best referrals; the rest get the crumbs. The top service technicians work on the best cars; the rest get the clunkers.

These strategies for distinction are vitally important for the company that wants its business to thrive and for the employee who wants her career to excel.

In their poignant book *The Simple Truths of Service: Inspired by Johnny the Bagger*, Ken Blanchard and Barbara Glanz tell the story of a young grocery bagger with Down syndrome who, through his creativity, gives customers more than they expect. He creates an enormous wave of enthusiasm and connection among his colleagues and his customers at the store where he works.[8]

I was with Ken Blanchard at a meeting in Lancaster, Pennsylvania, when he told the story of this creative young man who bagged groceries. He related that he had presented the same story to the staff of Petco Park, home stadium of baseball's San Diego Padres. At the end of a video for those employees prior to the grand opening of the park, he asked them, "Are you going to be a 'Johnny' tonight?"

Blanchard noted that throughout the baseball season, stadium managers and employees continued to ask one another, "Are you going to be a 'Johnny' tonight?"

In the first summer Petco Park was open, the team received more than 7,500 unsolicited letters from adoring fans who were compelled to take the time to write how they had been "blown away" (Blanchard's term) by the manner in which they were treated at the park.

The creativity of a single grocery bagger not only brought distinction to the specific store where he works but also inspired thousands of others to do likewise.

Why should you or I accept less from our organizations—or from ourselves?

Step Two: Pick a Point

Now that you know that every one of these specific items is an opening for you to create space between your organization and your competition, the next step is to review each point of contact to ascertain where you can develop differentiation.

Unfortunately, often the greatest areas of differentiation that most customers observe are merely in logos and color schemes. But does that have to be the case?

We know that Hertz is yellow, Avis is red, and National is green in the rental car world. But aren't there other meaningful ways to engage clients, ones that would help ensure repeat business? The last time I checked, a color on your sign would not accomplish that.

Enterprise Rent-A-Car has been clear about what it is—a company that rents automobiles. Yet when the company broke down the specific points of contact with customers, managers realized that at some point the renter has to obtain possession of the car. At other companies, customers must transport themselves to the rental locations, either at the airport or at a local office. Enterprise is known, of course, as the company that will "pick you up."

One of my favorite electronics retailers, Indianapolis-based H. H. Gregg, drove down its thinking regarding customer contact and recognized many sales revolved around large products that required both knowledgeable assistance prior to purchase and delivery following the decision. The customer's experience with delivery was one of the important points where contact was established and maintained on behalf of the organization.

Here's another example of driving it down, then picking a point: What ensues when customers pull into your parking lot? Have you even thought about it? Most businesses would say, "Well, good grief, they find a space and park!" Yet businesses that are dedicated to differentiate themselves will view such a basic action as an opportunity for distinction. They will ask highly detailed questions such as, "Exactly where will the customer park?" "How will they know it is the right spot?" And the best approach: "How can we be more creative about how we show the customer where to park?"

Recently, while working with top BMW car dealers in Europe, I realized how important this seemingly inconsequential point can become. Imagine pulling into the dealership to get your BMW serviced, only to discover a parking lot filled with . . . other BMWs. Where should you park yours?

It might seem small to you, but to your customer it can be a critical point. If the customer begins the experience feeling a bit confused, you haven't created the distinction you desire.

Joe Calloway is one of the nation's top professional speakers and a very close friend of mine. In his presentations, he often relates the story of Les Schwab Tires, a chain of about four hundred stores employing some seven thousand people in the western United States. I've heard Joe tell this story many times, and it never fails to elicit the audience response he desires.

Joe says to the audience, "I'm thinking of a company based in the Pacific Northwest that sells a commodity, yet they make it different." At this point, I've actually heard people call out, "Les Schwab!"

However, if Joe hasn't received his required response yet, he smiles and continues, "Let me give you a clue: tires." If they haven't already, the program participants familiar with Les Schwab shout the company's name.

Then Joe asks the magic question, "What makes their company different?" Members of the audience then wholeheartedly exclaim the answer.

Not only did Les Schwab and Enterprise and H. H. Gregg follow the first two steps of driving it down and picking a point, the company followed through with step three.

Step Three: Develop a Difference

ENTERPRISE RENT-A-CAR

In 1957 Jack Taylor launched Enterprise Rent-A-Car from the lower level of a St. Louis car dealership. Here's the story:

> Enterprise got its start by courting the airport passenger market. It could not afford to have space in the terminals, so their check-in facilities were located one or two blocks down the street. They countered this disadvantage by offering lower prices than Hertz and Avis. Their advertising campaign consisted of a photograph of a handsome male, well dressed and drinking a martini. The headline was, "Before I started using Enterprise Rent-A-Car, I lived with my mother." After they built some mass, they moved into the garage-rental market and switched their position to, "We'll pick you up." Their television commercials feature an automobile wrapped up like a gift package driving to the location of the person renting the car. The moral of the story is, regardless of how small your company is today, you can become a leader.[9]

By driving it down, picking a specific point—the manner in which the customer gets to the product—and developing a difference, Enterprise has grown into the largest rental car company in America.

Enterprise realized the creative opportunity for differentiation. If all the company did was to incrementally improve their airport locations against its competition at Hertz and Avis, Enterprise probably would have remained trapped by the Three Destroyers of Differentiation, and in all likelihood, the company would have collapsed.

As it is, you can almost visualize the creative moment in a brainstorming meeting when someone said, "Wait a minute! What if we go to our customers? What if we take the car to them?"

What differentiates Enterprise? You already know the answer: "At Enterprise, We Pick You Up."

By being creative—within the boundaries of their established clarity—Enterprise developed a powerful point of distinction.

H. H. GREGG

I can clearly remember being a small tot and Aunt Kak (my young, shorthand version of Katherine) taking me to a small appliance store on the north side of Indianapolis. As she shopped for a new refrigerator, this farm boy noted that the people from the big city were friendly and the selection seemed quite remarkable. I had never seen so many washing machines in one place in my life! We were at the original store of H. H. Gregg.

Fansy and H. H. Gregg started their store in 1955, offering washers, clothes dryers (and wringers), outdoor grills, and refrigerators like Aunt Kak was buying. Not long after, they added electronic products such as televisions.

When I originally wrote about H. H. Gregg in the first edition of this book, the company had about eighty-five stores in Alabama, Kentucky, Ohio, North Carolina, South Carolina, Tennessee, Florida, and Georgia, as well as in the Hoosier state. As proof the concepts we are discussing here really work, note that as of this writing H. H. Gregg is up to more than 190 locations.

Consider this important aspect: H. H. Gregg is opening stores in many communities at the very sites where the bankrupt Circuit City—a chain with a very similar product line—closed its locations.

What has made the difference? How can H. H. Gregg sell the same products at about the same prices and have remarkable growth at the same locations where another major retailer went bust?

H. H. Gregg believes it has an advantage because of its knowledge-able employees and low-price guarantee. In the first version of this book, I respectfully disagreed. However, I now realize *they* were right—and I underestimated the creativity the company was using in this regard.

As my wife and I entered the H. H. Gregg Superstore on 96th Street in Indianapolis, we were greeted with a smile and a wonderful opening comment when we informed our salesperson we were shopping for a washer and dryer: "Terrific! It's an important thing to do!"

When we asked for a little more information about why it was so important, the sincere response was, "Consider the combination of the importance of clean clothes, sanitary items in your home, the use of energy to accomplish this task, the environmental impact, and more! And as I am assuming you wear clothes every day—this is a purchase that impacts you all the time."

Well, I honestly didn't realize our selection of laundry equipment was such a monumental decision, but I was now really engaged!

We then received a basic lesson on the subject—and learned, for example, why selecting the proper size was of importance for saving on utility bills. As a result, we made our decision and felt we were well informed about our purchase. In addition, it struck me that if H. H. Gregg could deliver such extensive information about a washer and dryer, imagine what they could do for a more sophisticated piece of high-technology equipment.

However, promoting the fact that you have knowledgeable employees will not, in and of itself, make your company distinct. It's not exactly
as if your competitors are employing imbeciles, and every organization
says it has good people, even if it doesn't.

And sure, Gregg's low-price guarantee means it will match the
competition's price on equal items. But other major electronics retailers
offer the same promise, or a better one. So what makes the difference?

The additional creative and distinguishing point about H. H. Gregg
is its delivery to your home. If you purchase an item that is in stock
(prior to a reasonable evening cut-off time), the company will deliver it
to you the very same day. You can buy your new, enormous, flat-panel
television in the morning . . . and watch the big game in your home on
your new TV that very night.

As Andrei Codrescu, publisher of the online journal *Exquisite Corpse*,
said in an NPR commentary aired on *All Things Considered*, "We Americans don't like waiting. In the country of instant gratification, waiting is
unbearable. So we don't usually wait. We make phone calls and set up
meetings when the new batch of fries at McDonald's isn't out yet. We
don't like lines."[10]

How true. After we decide on the specific flat-panel TV, refrigerator,
or washer-dryer combination that we are willing to spend our hard-
earned money for, we want it now! And H. H. Gregg developed a point
of distinction by delivering it to us the same day as our purchase.

By the way, the delivery of our washer and dryer was executed perfectly, by a very friendly and knowledgeable crew who even conducted a
short "class" for my wife and me on how to use our new purchase. (And
there's an important point: if your customer doesn't know how to use the
advantages of your product or service, those advantages mean nothing
to them! Are you educating your customers and prospects as thoroughly
as they need to be?) We had a terrific experience at H. H. Gregg.

LES SCHWAB TIRES

After Joe Calloway asks the questions that move several in his audience to identify a tire retailer in the Pacific Northwest, he then inquires about the specific aspect that has created distinction for Les Schwab Tires. Those who have patronized this wonderful company yell, "They *run* to your car!"

At this point, those of us who hail from other parts of the country sit and listen a bit stunned as Joe smiles, nods, and asks, "Can the rest of you believe it? When you pull into their lot, they run . . . not walk quickly . . . not jog. They run to your car to serve you!"

Les Schwab Tires calls this "Sudden Service," and the company's locations execute it to near perfection.

Picture yourself needing a new set of tires and blocking out the better part of an afternoon to visit a few retailers in your area to get the best price. You know the size of tires your car must have; it's not as if you can negotiate a significant degree of variance on the requirements of this purchase as you might do in the case of a car or a house. You are also aware that there are a few major, notable manufacturers, so your range of choices is certainly more limited than if you were deciding where to dine that evening. And the fact is most of us choose from the two or three manufacturers that have better brand appeal than the others (such as Firestone, Goodyear, or Michelin), or we don't care what they put on the car—just make it the cheapest on which we can get by (this happens when there's not enough perceived brand differentiation to influence our purchasing choice).

When you pull into the XYZ Tire Store, you walk in, stand in line, and are gruffly greeted by someone who, from the look of his hands, has obviously been mounting and balancing tires all day. You pull out the slip of paper noting the size of the tires you need, and he pounds a computer keyboard and says, "Buddy, here's what we got in stock."

You note both the prices and his irritation when you say you are just checking around.

Next, at ABC Tire Store, you enter and find a clerk who smugly asks you if you have an appointment. When you respond in the negative and say that you are just checking around, she pounds a computer keyboard and says, "Here's what we have in stock. Would you like an appointment for installation?" You reiterate that you're just checking and proceed to your third and final destination.

Imagine that now you've pulled into Les Schwab Tires. You see a clean, smartly dressed professional, wearing a neat, pressed uniform, run to your car to serve you with a smile. Do you perceive at this instant that Les Schwab Tires possesses a point of distinction? Obviously it does!

I suggest that even if the tires and prices are the same, which they may or may not be, you will choose to do business with Les Schwab Tires because, as the Ebert Effect states, the company is different, and different is superior.

Creativity for an Organization

Here is a critical point: to achieve distinction, an organization does not have to become unique in *every* attribute of what it does. Instead, it has to be creative and develop a difference at a single point that is important to customers.

Les Schwab Tires still mounts Goodyears (and others) on their customers' cars, just like the competition. That is not what makes the company distinct in its industry.

The differentiation comes from becoming highly creative in at least one single, solitary aspect of its connection with the customer. Such companies have found a point of distinction that creates distance between them and their competitors.

And let's face it, by being the first in their business to take this approach, they make it impossible for their competition to duplicate it. If, all of a sudden, the employees at XYZ Tires started running for the cars, almost every prospective customer would think, "Wow. They must be in trouble. They're imitating—in fact, they're ripping off—Les Schwab!"

Creativity for the Individual Professional

For each of us on an individual level, the approach is exactly the same. What strategy can you implement that will create a point of distinction for you with your customers or within the organization—or both?

One manager I know and admire works with her staff to set team goals, and when they are accomplished, the office has a "Film Friday." They'll pop some popcorn and watch the DVD of a movie on the big screen in the conference room. This manager is beloved by her colleagues. (How many times is business really like all of those football analogies some managers frequently employ? Seldom do we get to act as if we're crossing the goal line and spiking the ball. This manager creates that thrill of achievement for her team.) Imagine being the next manager in that office and attempting to discontinue the practice.

Here's another example: the sales professional who can find a specific point of differentiation in the manner in which he makes a call is the one who will find his customers more receptive to his call—and his prospects more intrigued by what he has to say.

Motor, a magazine for professionals in the auto repair business, reports that some salespeople at auto service shops are remarkably enhancing their sales by taking a single, creative step. They simply ask their customers if they would like to add a first-rate trailer hitch to their vehicles.

According to the article, "Many vehicles equipped with trailer hitches were never built to tow a significant amount of weight. This means they present opportunities such as more frequent preventive maintenance due to accelerated wear, as well as opportunities to sell and install other accessories, such as suspension upgrades, transmission coolers and a host of others." Then these same sales professionals follow up with these customers to promote service on the trailers that these customers are now hitching up to their cars. These "trailers eventually need maintenance on exterior lighting, suspension and brakes, tires, axle alignment, etc."[11]

Reflect on what this means for a moment: every single day in just about every community in the country auto repair sales professionals talk to customers. How difficult is it to ask a question to determine whether the customer has ever considered hauling a boat? Or even the simpler, "Do you like to go fishing?"

Yes, It Really Is That Simple

Running to your car, picking you up with a rental, asking if you tow a boat—it just sounds too simplistic to be a real factor in creating differentiation, doesn't it? Yet here is the remarkable aspect of creative distinction: it really *is* that simple.

One representative for a dairy company used to call on Mom and Dad at their grocery store and wear a small flower in his lapel. Every time, without fail, that flower was there. Mom ordered more from him because he was "classy." Dad always noted he was a "real gentleman." As a young and impartial observer, I didn't notice much that was different about his milk and cheese. However, something as simple yet distinctive as a flower in his lapel created a small bit of competitive space for him.

President Nido Qubein of High Point University expanded on the clarity of the high-concept statement created by his team and then started getting highly creative.

Remember HPU's high concept? "At High Point University, every student receives an extraordinary education in an inspiring environment with caring people." The HPU team then developed innovative approaches for each segment of the high concept.

For example, how do you create the "inspiring environment" and deliver on that promise? One of the unique approaches was an "HPU Ice Cream Truck." Between classes, the truck—often accompanied by HPU's mascot, Panther—offers treats and encouragement to the students.

Inside the Student Center is a traditional college dining hall as well as a real Starbucks, a Chick-fil-A, and more. In addition, every student has access to a—ready for this?—campus concierge! Each student can utilize, without additional cost, the services of a concierge for wake-up calls, dry cleaning, shopping, movie tickets, and other offered services. More importantly, students are constantly exposed to a wide range of influential speakers, leaders, and authors.

At the end of the day, the point of all of this has to be to improve the education students receive and parents support. A *Good Morning America* report broadcast on September 20, 2008, noted that because of all of these creative elements that are establishing a distinct student experience, HPU's students have a higher motivation for academic excellence than those at other, less innovative institutions.

The results of these efforts? In the first edition of this book, I noted that High Point University was ranked by *U.S. News & World Report* in its "America's Best Colleges 2009" issue as the number one "up and coming" college among all comprehensive universities in the nation, and as the number three institution of all baccalaureate colleges in the South.

As the second edition went to press, Nido Qubein reported that during the past six years, HPU invested $700 million in adding faculty, constructing academic buildings, and providing state-of-the-art technology across campus, and grew its undergraduate enrollment by

175 percent (from 1,450 to 4,000). Additionally, the school expanded its graduate school from six to eleven programs, including masters and doctoral degrees. The physical campus expanded from 92 to 320 acres.

As a *Bloomberg Businessweek* article by Carol Matlack from the April 19, 2012, issue states, "Since becoming president in January 2005, [Qubein has] raised about $159 million in gifts and pledges, and has promised to kick in $11 million of his own money. There's more to come: new dorms, a health-sciences school, a college of pharmacy, a sports arena—all told, a planned $2.1 billion in improvements by 2020. All this in the middle of a depressed North Carolina mill town."

A Clear Message—Delivered Through Creativity

You can't have the clear message of being the "change" candidate and transmit that message in the same old manner as your competition. That's why the initial presidential campaign of Barack Obama employed new methods and integrated the second cornerstone into their efforts: creativity.

For example, the 2008 campaign successfully engaged supporters through an innovative approach to Twitter, which, back then, was a relatively new social networking service.

By Election Day 2008, the Obama campaign had 115,000 followers, the most of any account on the service at that time.

(Now, in a time when celebrities like Lady Gaga and Justin Bieber have more than 20,000,000 followers, it's amazing to think how relatively few followers put the presidential candidate at the top in 2008, isn't it? By mid-2012, President Obama was seventh in terms of Twitter followers—just ahead of Kim Kardashian, and right behind Britney Spears and Shakira.)

The initial Obama campaign also followed 119,000 Twitter members and used the service to drive interested members to the Obama website, where they could learn more about the campaign, as well as make a financial contribution to the candidate.

In addition, the ongoing status updates from the candidate (sent on an average of every other day for nineteen months) made those following feel both constantly and instantly connected in a manner never before seen in national politics.[12]

In addition, while the 2008 Obama campaign team strategically decided the youth vote was going to be vital to their success—something earlier campaigns from the Kennedys to McGovern and others had done, as well—they also found highly creative approaches to reach them. Young adults playing the video game *Burnout Paradise* on Xbox 360 would drive their virtual cars past a billboard noting "Early Voting Has Begun: Obama 2008."

"I can confirm that the Obama campaign has paid for in-game advertising in *Burnout Paradise*," Holly Rockwood, director of corporate communications at the game's publisher, Electronic Arts (EA), told the website GigaOM. She noted that EA regularly allows ad placements in their online games. "Like most television, radio, and print outlets, we accept advertising from credible political candidates," she said.

What she did not note, however, was that, unlike television, radio, and print, no political candidate had previously been creative enough to tap into the large audience of young voters that an EA game like *Burnout Paradise* could deliver.[13]

Obama's initial run for the White House was a terrific example of how difficult it is for any organization—even a well-funded campaign to obtain the most powerful position on earth—to become creative and innovative in any respective marketplace, even when they are clear about their mission.

And a major challenge faced by his re-election campaign in 2012 was identical to that encountered by other creative organizations and professionals: after we have grabbed attention and obtained success through our creative approaches, what can we do for a "second act"? In other words, if creativity helps us gain an initial win or advantage, how do we sustain a culture of innovation?

Here is an exercise that may help you meet that difficult challenge.

An Exercise

Part of the creativity you need to bring to your clarity may be discovered and executed in the manner in which you stay linked to your customers. Here is an exercise designed to develop your creativity regarding how you connect with colleagues and clients.

Create a list of the primary approaches and strategies being used by other professionals that you have observed in your field.

For example, if you are a manager, write down what other managers do as they provide leadership and direction to their people. If you are a salesperson, write down the sales approaches and techniques that are common in your industry.

My suggestion is to invest significant time in this exercise. You need to make a fairly complete list of the standard practices in your profession and for your position.

Now review and consider all of the approaches on your list. Carefully examine them.

Then, *don't* do them.

This idea may sound one-dimensional at first. If you really evaluate this little exercise, however, I believe you will begin to understand why it is at the heart of creativity. And, yes, I realize I'm overstating the case a bit here: if some of the approaches are moral absolutes—upholding equality, diversity, and respect for individuals, for example—you should obviously continue their application.

The main point I want you to consider is that imitation usually generates neither passion nor distinction. If you are copying from others—even if you are imitating the best in your field—you are propagating a "me too" approach that will continue to cast you adrift on the sea of sameness.

Perhaps It's Best Not to Pursue Best Practices

In the past several years, I have met too many "best practice junkies."

You may have worked for or with one of these types. They are always on the lookout for the next set of approaches they can imitate. They are practically groupies of the organizations that have become so dominant they are almost business clichés—Starbucks, Southwest, Apple, and Nordstrom are some obvious examples—and they use those practices as their business bible.

They become so enthralled with a creative best practice from another organization, they often neglect to evaluate whether that approach is applicable for their situation. Of course, for many professionals, it's much easier to imitate someone else's best practices than to creatively develop their own.

Back in September 1993, Dr. Jac Fitz-enz, founder of the Saratoga Institute in Santa Clara, California, illuminated some of the primary problems with best practices in the professional journal *Human Resource Planning*. "Many business articles focused on 'best practice' firms result in misleading conclusions regarding business success," Dr. Fitz-enz stated. He went on:

Let's look at some of the problem areas, starting with the basics. For example: what does "best" mean? This is a highly subjective, nonspecific question. Who says what's best? On what basis do they say it's best? For whom is it best? In what way is it best? In searching for answers, we may fall victim to such fallacies as the "halo effect." We read about Company X, and the article says they're absolutely great at such and so. And it's true; they are. But, in the absence of a sufficiently sharp, specific focus, the reader may buy into the notion that they're great at everything. Nobody is.[14]

What Fitz-enz is saying supports, from organizational and personal perspectives, our approach in putting clarity before creativity.

Pick your specific focus and be abundantly clear about that first. Then develop creative approaches that build distinction in precisely defined areas. We already know that no organization and no professional is going to be great at everything. Dr. Fitz-enz continued:

Another dangerous pitfall is the "small sample extension." Somebody looks at a few companies—and extrapolates the outcomes to infinity. Not only is a "best practice" subjective—it's transitory. It changes faster than dress styles. What was best last month may not be best today. In fact, by the time you read about it, it may be passé. It may even have gone from being right to being downright wrong.[15]

"Good to . . . Mediocre"?

Now here is a spot in the original book where I stirred a bit of controversy, and I continue to believe this point—and even more fervently—to this day. However, I approach the subject with the understanding that it is where I might get into trouble with some readers.

Jim Collins's book *Good to Great* is a mega-best seller.[16] It is a "must read" in the business community, and its concepts are discussed ad nauseum at conferences, seminars, and conventions. Its teaching has been accepted as gospel at many organizations.

While I am appreciative of Collins's dedication to his research and impressed by his extraordinary accomplishments, I nevertheless believe several of the significant points he selected to exemplify what makes a company "great" are simply incorrect. This, I would suggest, renders some of the book's business principles unhelpful for organizations and individuals attempting to create distinction.

In the book, Collins selects eleven companies by means of the statistical models he created, and the extensive research conducted by his team. One of the chosen few is Circuit City, a bankrupt company that died a slow death as a bricks-and-mortar retailer because it evidently did not know how to differentiate from a competitor such as Best Buy or deliver like the previously mentioned H. H. Gregg.

(According to CircuitCity.com, the "Circuit City" name "including intellectual property [trademarks, patents, etc.], domain names, customer lists, contact information, other customer basic information and other assets" were sold to Systemax Inc. on May 19, 2009. The new owners currently retail popular electronics from the site.)

To remind you of Circuit City's history, here is an excerpt from an article on Forbes.com dated February 26, 2008:

> Circuit City reported a $207 million loss in its fiscal third quarter and anticipates a "modest loss" in the fourth quarter, the period that included the bulk of the crucial holiday-shopping season. The company has floundered after experiencing a devastating third-quarter loss, reported last December 21, of $207.3 million. The losses came after Circuit City fired 3,400 experienced workers to replace them with lower-waged workers.[17]

That meant customers of this "great" company had a difficult time during an all-important Christmas rush finding employees who knew what they were doing and could answer questions.

This led to Circuit City announcing later in 2008 that they were closing about 20 percent of their stores and firing thousands of additional
workers. "The weakened environment has resulted in a slowdown of
consumer spending,"[18] said James A. Marcum, vice chairman and acting
president and CEO.

However, I suggested in the original version of this book that
the primary problem wasn't the economy—it was the inability of the
"great" Circuit City to create distinction.

Don Reisinger, columnist for C-net News, explains it this way:

Why is it so hard for everyone discussing Circuit City's Chapter
11 filing and New York Stock Exchange stock suspension to tell
the world what really happened with this company?

No, Circuit City isn't dying because of the credit crunch, and
there's no way we can blame its demise on the preferential treat-
ment competitors like Best Buy are receiving. And we certainly
can't blame it on the online-retail industry.

Knowing that Circuit City's executives over the past eight
years have single-handedly ruined any prospect for growth,
thanks to questionable decisions and poor management of
company assets, the current team of executives wants to blame
everyone else but themselves.

The numbers and the financial data speak for themselves;
the only reason Circuit City is in ruin today is because of the
company's executives. After all, Best Buy is competing in the
same environment, and that company has performed extremely
well. Why couldn't the sector's most prominent company from
years ago have done the same?

It's unfortunate, but there's no saving Circuit City now. The
game is over, and the retailer has lost.[19]

Yet in *Good to Great* Collins praises Circuit City's then-CEO not only for his corporate approach and vision but also for how he selected and managed the members of his team.

In the years since the original publication of this book, however, I have realized on a personal basis how an author can be deceived about organizations he is involved with, either through his research or via friendships. Such was the case with my earlier writing about Obsidian Enterprises.

It has now become apparent, just like investors in other companies that the same individuals managing Obsidian also operated, I too was misled about the performance and results of a company and persons I wrote about in a positive manner. While it is easy to note that other distinguished media outlets—from CNBC to the *Indianapolis Business Journal*—were simultaneously heaping praise on the company and its leaders as well, what I wrote is solely my responsibility, and I was wrong.

However, the failure of both the individuals and the organizations had zero to do with the principles being advocated here. Instead, a solid case could be made that their rejection of the implementation of these very steps to create distinction and secure organizational success in part precipitated the demise of the company and careers of its leaders.

Things have also fared poorly, too, at some of the other *Good to Great* companies. While it is an ethical matter, and not one based upon sheer economics and management, it would be highly difficult for me to ever proclaim Philip Morris as a "great" company. When the result of extended use of your product results in the illness or death of your best customers, how can it be argued that the company is "great"? However, Collins reported in *Good to Great* that his selection "stuck much closer to the tobacco business, in large part because they loved that business." He stated he was "surprised" by their "passion" and notes an interview with a board member who "proudly puffed away" during their conversation.

I just disagree. When your product has been proven to be a legitimate threat to kill your customers, you are disqualified in my book from greatness.

Although it is only one aspect of a public company's success, Walgreens' share price has shrunk while supposedly "non-Great" CVS stock has grown. As of the end of April 2012, Walgreens' stock was down 13.5 percent for the past year. CVS, however, was up more than 24 percent in the same time period. While *Good to Great* touted Walgreens in 2001 as the winner over CVS—and states that "great companies, for the most part, have always been great"—by 2008 Walgreens was under intense pressure from shareholders to match the results of its major competitor.

"Even the best of companies at times have to change their business model,"said Gregory Wasson, Walgreens president and chief operating officer.[20]

Gillette was acquired by Proctor & Gamble—not one of the "great" companies of the book, which perhaps begs the question: how is a "non-great" company so successful it is able to simply buy a "great" one? Pitney Bowes—with a core product helping customers deliver junk mail—only recently concluded, after eighty-five acquisitions, that the company should "re-brand" itself and consider a "whole brand" philosophy, meaning, of course, their clarity could use some work.

Perhaps the best thing about *Good to Great* was the title. Or, as stated above, best practices aren't always best.

In an interview, business guru Tom Peters stated:

The companies that Jim calls great have performed well. I wouldn't deny that for a minute, but they haven't led anybody anywhere. I don't give a damn whether Microsoft is around fifty years from now. Microsoft set the agenda in the world's most important industry at a critical period of time, and that to me is leadership, not the fact that you are able to stay alive until your beard is 200 feet long.[21]

In the book, Collins also proclaims, "In fact, leaders that go from good to great start not with 'where' but with 'who.' They start by getting the right people on the bus, the wrong people off the bus, and the right people in the right seats."[22]

Really? I assume you are one of the "right people." Here's my question: Would you get on a bus if you did not know where it was going?

And note one of the primary corporate examples the book employed to exemplify the "right people on the bus"—financial giant Fannie Mae. Even well before the September 7, 2008, move by the Federal Housing Finance Agency to place Fannie Mae under federal conservatorship, here was an organization the *Washington Post* reported in 2004 had "maintained a corporate culture that emphasized stable earnings *at the expense of accurate financial disclosures* [emphasis added]."[23]

Following the federal takeover, the Fannie Mae website reported its "Board of Directors no longer has the power or duty to manage, direct or oversee the business and affairs of Fannie Mae." The CEO and CFO of Fannie Mae resigned, and the *Wall Street Journal* reported in June 2008 that two former CEOs received their personal home loans at below market rates from Countrywide Financial—when Fannie Mae was the biggest purchaser of Countrywide's mortgages.

When you examine the financial debacle in the mortgage industry that precipitated an extraordinary economic crisis in the United States and the world, any reasonable observer has to include this organization as one of the significant culprits. So I ask you—were these the "right people" in the "right seats"?

On another front, my colleague, friend, and fellow Speakers Round-table member Charlie Plumb was a prisoner of war in North Vietnam for nearly six years. He has stated on many occasions that the section in *Good to Great* regarding the assertion of Admiral James Stockdale that the "optimists" were the ones who "didn't make it out" was the opinion of only one POW—Stockdale himself.

The book calls this "The Stockdale Paradox" and says, "You must never confuse faith that you will prevail in the end—which you can never afford to lose—with the discipline to confront the most brutal facts of your current reality, whatever they might be."

However, as Plumb related to me, the problem is that it seems to him the text is derisive of those who were the optimists—a category in which Plumb squarely places himself.

Charlie Plumb, author of *I'm No Hero*, states that it is impossible to make the choice to become an optimist—which the *Encarta Diction-ary* defines as "somebody who tends to feel hopeful and positive about future outcomes"—without realistically understanding the set of cir-cumstances about which you are optimistic. True optimists confront the facts and choose to feel hopeful, and according to Plumb, they were the ones who dealt with the extreme challenges the POWs faced most productively. Pessimists confronted the same set of facts, and came to a less positive attitude.

In a later work, Collins suggests—I'm paraphrasing him here—that as long as an organization can innovate at roughly the same pace as its competition, execution is all that truly matters. In one dialogue with Cisco Chairman John Chambers, Collins asked the leader of the technol-ogy giant to choose one strategy: innovation or execution.

Chambers later related that he chose "execution" simply because it was Collins asking the question, and the smart CEO could guess what the author's choice of answers would be. Chambers also said, otherwise, he would have selected "innovation."

The question we should pose is: *why choose at all?*

It should be easy to recognize that creativity without execution is managerial masturbation. It is creating corporate fantasies to please no one other than ourselves.

Execution without creativity is excruciatingly boring. It ensures we never rise above the sea of sameness in which most organizations and individual professionals are adrift.

> *Execution without creativity is boring.*

To try to choose one *or* the other—especially in an attempt to create distinction—is sheer folly. In other words, a question like the one Collins asked makes no sense in today's marketplace. Every organization and individual should be focusing upon the "and"—creativity *and* innovation—not the "or."

My point is this: there are a myriad of concepts presented by a multitude of business books. Whether the point is "The Stockdale Paradox" or getting the "right people on the bus," the fact remains that no one has truly defined a formula that can always make a company "great."

However, my research and my personal experience have convinced me that organizations that clearly and creatively seek to differentiate—and raise their performance to a level that creates distinction—will naturally become superior to inconspicuous competitors.

The very day I initially wrote this segment a few years ago, Starbucks was announcing lower-than-expected earnings, and its chairman, Howard Schultz, cautioned that the company was entering a difficult period. Starbucks sales had fallen, as had store traffic.

"The wheels have really come off of this train," RBC Capital Markets analyst Larry Miller told Reuters at the time, noting his surprise at the warning. "It's amazing how fast business has derailed. If sales are down mid-single digits, that is a rapid erosion."[24]

The point is, some of the differentiated companies identified in this book may still encounter difficult times. It's quite possible that the executives and managers I tout here will not deliver the results their colleagues or shareholders anticipate.

So if a top-flight, creative, and differentiated company like Starbucks—or like the companies in *Good to Great*—can encounter challenges, why should you expend significant effort to become distinct?

It is true, you may very well take a tumble in difficult times. Nevertheless, if you have made the effort to create distinction, you have begun a defense against being knocked out. When the economy tightens and the market shrinks, a differentiated company may not have gross earnings or net profits as substantial as before. Individual professionals—especially those with compensation tied to commissions or revenue—may experience a considerable decline in income. Yet in many situations, their competitors may be going out of business entirely. Just ask yourself, how much lower could your company go if it wasn't distinctive?

Differentiation is like a vaccine for your career and your company.

There's No One "Right Way"

Initial research on Starbucks a few years ago indicated people weren't dumping Starbucks to drink coffee someplace else. People just weren't spending as much on lattes when gasoline costs hovered around four dollars a gallon.

Starbucks reported a 97 percent drop in profit in the third quarter of 2008, but that figure was primarily due to charges associated with restructuring. What was overlooked was that, even with the challenging economy in 2008, Starbucks brought in $10.4 billion, a 10 percent increase over 2007![25]

In the original edition, I wrote, "I would be willing to place my bet on Starbucks—when average consumers find more change in their pockets in a better economic cycle, they will enhance their orders from a tall to a grande or vente."

When "great" isn't good enough . . . distinction is the game changer.

Guess what? In the fifty-two-week cycle from May 1, 2011, to April 30, 2012, Starbucks share price has almost doubled.

You do not need to change everything about how you do business to create distinction.

Start by walking through your list of points of contact with customers, reframing and redefining how you perceive each moment of interaction. From these new perspectives, you can then begin to create specific points of differentiation with your customers. By developing your professional laundry list from the exercise—and recognizing that if these practices are the industry standard, then they will almost always fail to create distinction for you—you are taking an important first step in disciplining yourself as a professional to develop differentiated methods and tactics.

As we learned from the "Ebert Effect," different is not just good, different is *superior*. Creating distinction is what you must do when "great" isn't good enough to grow your business.

It Shouldn't Be a Secret

However, in addition to the extraordinary benefits it spawns, this second cornerstone also presents a challenge. Even when you are executing to perfection, all the creativity in the world won't do you or your organization any good if you keep your new, compelling ideas a secret.

It is time to shine! You now have a powerful story to tell. The next chapter will focus on why it is so important to tell it, and outline how to do that in today's world.

Executive Summary

I.   The second of the Four Cornerstones of Distinction is *creativity*.

    A. In most companies, the creative potential far exceeds creative performance.

        1. Most of us truly believe we are not creative.

    B. Creativity is an "instinct to produce."

        1. Our goal is to be creative, so we can produce efforts that create distinction.

II. Creativity must be second, following clarity.

    A. Creativity without clarity is devoid of distinction.

        1. Even the most creative artists respect the baseline of the restrictions of the format they have selected.

           a. Novels require words; songs require music.

        2. Therefore, the creativity we are going to generate will always be grounded within the clarity we have developed from the first cornerstone.

III. Three steps to creativity

    A. Believe you are creative.

        1. Once you believe you aren't creative, you stop attempting originality.

        2. The first step to creativity is simply believing you are creative.

    B. Expose yourself to stimulus.

        1. Creative people expose themselves to stimulating—and even controversial—thoughts from books, movies, and other forms of art.

        2. They open up their minds to innovation by building the spirit necessary to create.

    C. Understand that creativity is synergistic.

        1. "None of us is as smart as all of us."

        2. Brainstorm with other bright, stimulating people to grow

creativity through synergy.

IV. Stimulating productive creativity

    A. Drive it down.

        1. Break down the points of contact between your organization (or you) and your customer.

        2. Each of these points provides an opportunity for you to creatively differentiate yourself.

    B. Pick a point.

        1. Choose one of these specific points of contact and practice creativity.

        2. Enterprise Rent-A-Car created distinction by picking the point of how their customers acquired the rental car.

    C. Develop a difference.

        1. Positively exploit that area you have selected.

        2. Enterprise exploited the point by differentiating themselves from their competitors by picking up their customers, instead of having them go to the rental car location.

           a. "At Enterprise, we pick you up!"

        3. Other examples include H. H. Gregg's same-day delivery of appliances and Les Schwab Tires' "sudden service" of running to a customer's car.

V. Creativity that is congruent with your clarity

    A. High Point University developed extraordinary creativity based upon the clarity described earlier.

        1. For example, the "inspiring environment" promised was achieved with a variety of methods, including a campus truck of ice cream and bottled water for students between classes, and outstanding programs of motivating speakers.

        2. A campus concierge handles wake-up calls, dinner reservations, and dry cleaning for students.

           a. The result is that HPU was named by *U.S. News & World*

Report as the "number one up and coming" institution of higher learning in the nation.

VI. "Best practices" aren't always "best."

    A. Your creativity is vital. Following trends, often called "best practices," can have unintended consequences.

        1. Some become so enthralled with what marquee companies like Starbucks and Apple are doing, they believe doing the same thing will have a similar effect upon their organization or career.

    B. The dangerous "small sample extension"

        1. Research proves that extrapolating these best-practice outcomes beyond their scope in this hyper-changing marketplace often fails to produce the desired results.

    C. The fallacies of *Good to Great*

        1. Jim Collins's bestseller selected eleven "great" companies:

        2. One of them, Circuit City, is now in bankruptcy.

        3. Gillette was acquired by a "non-great" company.

        4. Philip Morris's products can cause its best customers to become ill or die.

        5. Fannie Mae is at the center of the nation's financial and housing market collapse.

        6. Walgreens is making significant changes because of the larger success of its "non-great" competitor CVS.

        7. "The people on the bus are more important than where the bus is going" is clearly wrong!

            a. Would *you* get on a bus if you didn't know where it was going?

            b. High performers respond to clear and creative visions.

VII. Distinction is the only approach that generates greatness with longevity.

A. While some of the companies touted in *Create Distinction,* or others that have developed differentiation, may achieve lesser results depending upon the market or choices by their leaders, true distinction is like a vaccine for your career and your company.

B. Organizations and professionals that clearly and creatively seek to differentiate themselves—and raise their performance to the level that creates distinction—will naturally become superior to inconspicuous competitors.

   1. There is no single "right way" to do business.

   2. Any "guru" that attempts to define such a "right way" is simply misleading the reader.

   3. However, those professionals and organizations that follow the Four Cornerstones will naturally find themselves creating space from the pack.

   4. And as we learned earlier from the Ebert Effect, "different *is* superior."

Action Steps, Questions, and Ideas

- What is every point of contact that a customer has with you or your organization? Make an extremely detailed listing.

- Select one of these points of contact. Then create five innovative strategies for enhancing the quality of the contact with your customer at that stage.

- Select one challenge your organization faces in creating distinction in the marketplace. Then attempt to redefine the challenge from another perspective. Write down your new approach to an old problem.

SEVEN

THE THIRD CORNERSTONE:

COMMUNICATION

I was about to give a presentation for one of my best clients at the Doubletree Hotel in Overland Park, Kansas. As I was entering the meeting room for my speech, the banner of another organization holding a conference across the hall stopped me in my tracks. I looked at it with amazement.

I tapped the shoulder of an executive of the company sponsoring my program, pointed out the poster, and said, "That may be the most foolish phrase I have ever seen at a business meeting."

The theme of the other organization's conference was "Sales Cure Everything!"

I could not believe the organization's ignorance and the erroneous information they were communicating to their team. Sales do not cure everything—not by a long shot.

If your organization isn't serving your customers well, do more sales cure that problem? Of course not.

If your company cannot retain good employees because it lacks the clarity necessary to create distinction, do more sales cure that? Absolutely not.

If you cannot make your product stand out in the marketplace, and you slice your price—selling more, but earning significantly less—does that cure everything for you and your organization? You know it doesn't.

If you fail to communicate what your organization is about, what it stands for, or what makes you clearly compelling individually as a professional, will hawking more of your stuff cause your challenges in communication to evaporate? Please don't deceive yourself into thinking that it might.

What Sales Do Accomplish

Here's what sales will accomplish: if you are a commission-based professional enduring a slow month, more sales make the pain of that period easier to handle. If you are judged on the revenue you generate, more sales will temporarily prevent your managers from calling you on the carpet. If you lead a public company, more sales may avert your share price from falling for a bit. If you own a small business, more sales may briefly keep your banker at bay.

However, while more sales may ease the symptoms of a current situation or keep it on life support, more sales definitely do not cure anything.

Sales—perhaps—*extend* things. Sales don't alleviate your problems but may mean you can suffer them for a longer period.

Differentiation and Distinction Cure What Ails You

Creating distinction is the strategy that takes an ailing organization or career and gets it back on its feet and in the race.

Distinction has taken organizations from being in corporate intensive care to winning the business equivalent of Olympic gold. And differentiation—and the resulting personal and organizational distinction—just does not occur without compelling communication.

What would have happened if, during the darkest days at Harley-Davidson—immediately after the thirteen senior executives had purchased the company back from AMF in 1981—those leaders had communicated to their team this message: "Ladies and gentlemen, just focus on sales. *Sales cure everything!*"?

The company was in an incredibly difficult situation. Product quality had become a joke, and the Super Glide bike had a horrible reputation. Harley dealers and their customers, ignored and abused by the previous regime, were now bolting to other manufacturers. Instead of saying, "Sales cure everything," the Harley executives announced that "The Eagle Soars Alone" and dedicated themselves and their company to becoming the distinct leader in their market by reconnecting and intensely communicating with their current customers and making a compelling case for prospects.

You know how that story turned out, right?

Therein lies perhaps the most important point. Lots of companies seek a superior position in the marketplace, just as Harley aspired to claim. However, you remember Harley not because you happen to recall the price of the acquisition paid to the former owner by the management team. Nor do most of us specifically remember what Harley shares were trading for when it returned as a public company a few years later, compared to its current valuation.

What we remember is the *story* that Harley communicated.

To more thoroughly understand why, you have to master the third Cornerstone of Distinction—communication.

This chapter examines:

- How you can exchange your information with customers in a manner that is compelling and engaging
- Why creating emotional impact is vitally important in today's culture
- How to link with clients through the "power of story"
- A simple "three-act" structure for constructing and conveying your narrative so that it builds distinction for you in the marketplace

Information or Connection?

You and your organization probably have access to reams of data about what your customers are purchasing and why. If you are an entrepreneur with a small business, you likely belong to a trade association that can offer you a similar quantity of research.

The problem is, only a fraction of these assessments will provide real insight into how you can take your clarity—now combined with creativity toward building unique and highly specific points of differentiation between you and your competitors—and turn your information into communication that truly connects with your customers and prospects.

We tend to abdicate our aspirations of profound customer rapport solely to companies that create significant sensory responses, such as Harley-Davidson and other previously mentioned organizations such as Apple. Most of us in business stand amazed at the bond and loyalty inspired by those select few. Harley-Davidson customers are willing to tattoo its logo on their bodies. That is a connection almost beyond description.

Not coincidentally, many of us can tell the stories of these companies. We know how Harley came back from the brink of extinction. We know about the return of Steve Jobs to the company he helped found in a garage, about Herb Kelleher creating an airline on a cocktail napkin, and about Fred Smith writing a master's thesis about the company he wanted to establish.

Here's the challenge: we are enthralled by *their* stories, but we tend to dismiss our *own*.

That, in my opinion, is a big mistake. It would be a profound blunder to presume only a select few companies possess either the history or the ability to engender stories that can create a connection with customers and prospects. Every organization and every professional has a compelling story.

For most of us, though, the problem is the story is still waiting to be told.

Legendary computer scientist Alan Kay, formerly of Disney and now head of the Viewpoints Research Institute, has said: "Why was Solomon recognized as the wisest man in the world? Because he knew more stories—proverbs—than anyone else. Scratch the surface in a typical boardroom and we're all just cavemen with briefcases, hungry for a wise person to tell us stories."[1]

Everyone loves a story. }

I realized this firsthand when I was asked to return to my hometown of Crothersville and give a lecture for school teachers and administrators. I have to admit that well before the program even started, I was already feeling scared to death. Sitting in the front row was one of my former teachers.

Part of the problem I experienced was caused by my memories of the tremendous crush that I had had during my elementary school years on this then-cute, petite, very young teacher. On my return home, I naturally looked forward to seeing her again. However, the image in my mind of her was of the way she looked when I was in the third grade. Imagine my shock in seeing her now, at sixty-five years old, and noticing that her stretch pants had no choice.

Of course, she was just as shocked . . . standing in front of her was not the skinny, bespectacled eight-year-old kid with the "burr" haircut of her memories. It was a mid-forties guy with a mustache and a bit of a potbelly.

Being more than just a little nervous, I decided to start my presentation with a very standard question many speakers and authors ask to begin a lecture to teachers. "Let's start by having you tell me," I said, "what you believe is the biggest problem for educators in today's world."

I thought I knew the answers these teachers were going to give, because I had rehearsed it so thoroughly in my program preparation. Naturally, their biggest problems were going to be:

1. Disciplining the students
2. Encouraging the involvement of parents
3. Drug or alcohol use
4. Funding challenges in education

Imagine my surprise when my former teacher raised her hand and declared, "Scott, I believe the biggest problem in education today is *Sesame Street*."

I immediately responded with a profound, "Huh?"

Calmly, my former educator asked me, "Scott, who taught you your ABCs?"

I answered truthfully, "Well, my mother and my grandmother."

"Of course," she said. "However, for the last thirty years, young people have been taught their ABCs by Big Bird and Bert and Ernie. That means they arrive on the steps of this school for their very first day of formal instruction expecting to be entertained as they are educated."

"Wow!" I thought. Then I realized, my elementary school teacher was still teaching me.

In this age, when most of us have grown up learning our ABCs from Big Bird and Cookie Monster rather than through the disciplined rote and repetition of a former time, our fervent desire for a wise person or distinct organization to tell us stories continues to expand.

We are starved for stories.

The Powerful Story of a Very Senior Citizen

Throughout Barack Obama's 2008 presidential campaign, he relied on compelling stories to connect with his audiences. However, there is no better example than a story he related to the hundreds of thousands in Grant Park in Chicago (and the millions watching globally) on election night. Even though he had received more than 65 million votes on that historic day, the new president-elect concentrated on the story of just one solitary voter.

> This election had many firsts and many stories that will be told for generations. But one that's on my mind tonight is about a woman who cast her ballot in Atlanta. She's a lot like the millions of others who stood in line to make their voice heard in this election except for one thing—Ann Nixon Cooper is 106 years old.
>
> She was born just a generation past slavery—a time when there were no cars on the road or planes in the sky; when someone like her couldn't vote for two reasons: because she was a woman and because of the color of her skin.
>
> And tonight, I think about all that she's seen throughout her century in America—the heartache and the hope, the struggle and the progress, the times we were told that we can't, and the people who pressed on with that American creed: Yes, we can.
>
> At a time when women's voices were silenced and their hopes dismissed, she lived to see them stand up and speak out and reach for the ballot. Yes, we can.
>
> When there was despair in the dust bowl and depression across the land, she saw a nation conquer fear itself with a

New Deal, new jobs, and a new sense of common purpose. Yes, we can.

When the bombs fell on our harbor and tyranny threatened the world, she was there to witness a generation rise to greatness and a democracy was saved. Yes, we can.

She was there for the buses in Montgomery, the hoses in Birmingham, a bridge in Selma, and a preacher from Atlanta who told a people that "we shall overcome." Yes, we can.

A man touched down on the Moon, a wall came down in Berlin, a world was connected by our own science and imagination. And this year, in this election, she touched her finger to a screen, and cast her vote, because after 106 years in America, through the best of times and the darkest of hours, she knows how America can change. Yes, we can.[2]

Note that Barack Obama could have said, "Look, in this country we've had slavery, depression, wars, moon landings, and a whole lot more. This night is going to go down in history, too.

"Now . . . let's get to work."

However, his viewing of these monumental events through the eyes of a single individual who earlier in her life could not even cast a ballot because of her race, then because of her gender, presents all of these chapters of our nation's history in a more personal—and powerful—dimension.

Understanding Story

A significant voice on the subject of the power of stories and myth is Joseph Campbell. His work is one of the most significant texts available on how to craft compelling, emotionally connecting stories. Campbell's work from the 1940s, *The Hero with a Thousand Faces*, has influenced generations of storytellers, including *Star Wars* creator George Lucas, who stated that his blockbuster series of films was shaped by Campbell's approach.[3]

One of Campbell's main points is that for a story to be compelling, the hero cannot begin the narrative as the winner. In other words, a story about your professional or personal efforts—or about the growth and development of your organization—cannot begin with your success.

The Harley-Davidson story is compelling in great part because the company was on the brink of disaster. Apple started in the garage, *not* as a darling of Wall Street; therefore, the return of Steve Jobs as the company was on the brink of extinction makes the story of its success and becoming, perhaps, the world's leading organization an even more gripping narrative.

Campbell said, "A hero is someone who has given his or her life to something bigger than oneself."[4] Only through trials and tribulations—being tested and defeated and *then* rising up to conquer—do we really become heroes.

In Homer's *Odyssey*, Ulysses is not a hero at the beginning of the book. It is through facing his trials and challenges that he *becomes* one. In the New Testament, one way in which his followers recognized Jesus as divine was through his ability to endure and resist varied forms and incarnations of temptation. The impact of *The Odyssey* or the New Testament would be greatly diminished without the tribulations their heroes successfully overcame.

We are story junkies. We get hooked on good stories. They can be scripted, as soap operas have demonstrated for decades before millions of viewers (and listeners, in the days of radio) on a daily basis. The stories can be reality-based, as *Survivor* and the glut of imitators that have followed have clearly proved.

And they can even be grounded in the business world. (Think *Undercover Boss, Shark Tank, The Apprentice*, and more.)

The Benefits of Story

Mary E. Boyce, professor in the Department of Management and Business at Whitehead College, University of Redlands, California, wrote in the *Journal of Organizational Change*:

> Shared storytelling has a number of applications that warrant consideration by organizational members, managers, and practitioners. These are:
>
> a. Expressing the organizational experience of members or clients;
>
> b. Confirming the shared experiences and shared meaning of organizational members and groups within the organization;
>
> c. Orienting and socializing new organizational members;
>
> d. Amending and altering the organizational reality;
>
> e. Developing, sharpening, and renewing the sense of purpose held by organizational members;
>
> f. Preparing a group (or groups) for planning, implementing plans, and decision making in line with shared purposes; and
>
> g. Co-creating vision and strategy.[5]

Boyce's article addresses the benefits of communication through story from an internal organizational perspective. I would suggest the power of story must also be applied on the exterior, so that the communication through a compelling and powerful story creates a persuasive bond between you and your customers, clients, and prospects.

To see how influential this can become, let's look at an older story about the Macintosh computers from Apple.

Your Customers, Your Sales Force

The cover story from *Businessweek* back in mid-May 2008, written by Peter Burrows, disclosed that a large and rapidly growing number of employees in thousands of companies were requesting Apple's Macs on the job rather than standard-issue Windows-based machines.

According to Burrows, one reason that Macs are not even more prevalent in the corporate world is that Apple has no sales force dedicated to marketing its products to businesses, as the competition at Dell and HP does, for example. Yet because the millions of dedicated fans in the "cult of Mac" (of which I am a proud member) know the company's story and are enthusiastic about retelling it, Apple's customers have become a de facto sales team for the company.

Burrows writes:

Soon after Michele Goins became chief information officer at Juniper Networks in February, she decided to respond to the growing chorus of Mac lovers among the networking company's 6,100 employees. For years, many had used Apple's computers at home and clamored for them in the office as well. So she launched a test, letting 600 Juniper staffers use Macs instead of the standard-issue PCs that run Microsoft's Windows operating system. As long as the extra support costs aren't too high, she plans to open the floodgates. "If we opened it up today, I think 25 percent of our employees would choose Macs," she says.

Burrows goes on:

Funny thing is she [Goins] has *never received a single sales call* from Apple. . . . It's a people's revolution, of sorts, with workers increasingly pressing their employers to let them use Macs in the office. . . . Mark Slaga, chief information officer of Dimension Data, a large computer services firm based in suburban Johannesburg, says he has received twenty-five e-mails recently from employees who want permission to use Macs at work. So far he has refused, because he doesn't want to hire people to provide Mac tech support, but "it'll happen someday," he concedes. *"Steve Jobs doesn't need a sales force because he already has one: employees like the ones in my company* [italics added]."[6]

Look at what has happened since the article was written. A Dimensional Research study has revealed Apple's iOS to be the preferred platform for mobile connections in the corporate world, with 78 percent saying there are twice as many mobile devices in the workplace in 2012 as in 2010.

Wouldn't you like it if your customers also became a sort of "voluntary sales force"?

It can occur only if your clients are able to communicate your story for you. And let's face it, if *you* aren't telling your story, you can't expect *them* to do so!

Again, it would be easy to dismiss this as an impossible phenomenon to duplicate without a hip product like the iPhone or MacBook Air, but that would be an incorrect assumption.

It isn't difficult to find many other companies creating this kind of enthusiasm in their customers. From Levenger's, for fountain pens and upscale tools for readers, to Carl Nielsen, my car salesman at Dreyer & Reinbold BMW in Indianapolis, I have often been an advocate of large and small organizations—and of individual professionals as well—and so have you! The unifying elements among all of these people and companies are that they are differentiated and have distinctive stories to tell—stories they have told me and that I have repeated.

My hope is that the discussion in this chapter is moving you toward understanding the importance of telling your story. The companies I've mentioned are all market leaders. Individuals like Carl Nielsen are top performers. They have attained distinction not only in their respective industries but also throughout the entire marketplace.

And they *all* tell their story. I call this a *clue.*

Customers seek that magical quality of distinction. As we have already discovered, distinction is developed by organizations and professionals that first develop *clarity* about what they are—followed by *creativity* in their approach—and that then *communicate* their story in a compelling manner.

It is no coincidence that these organizations that we are tired of hearing about—Southwest, Starbucks, Apple, and so forth—are the ones most frequently telling their stories in a precise and compelling manner.

Why is it so difficult to find other examples? I suggest the reason is that so few organizations or individuals in business today understand the basics of telling the compelling story.

The Three-Act Format of Storytelling

If you believe that you aren't a storyteller, well, you probably also said in an earlier chapter that you aren't creative, didn't you?

You don't have to be a natural storyteller. You just have to be interested and committed to your story.

- You need to be interested not only in your own story but also in the power of a story to convey information, emotion, and understanding.
- You must be intrigued by how you can leverage your uniqueness into connectivity with your customers and colleagues through the presentation of your unique story.
- You have to be committed to telling your story.

In today's world it's not enough to create the story. You have to be committed to conveying it *repeatedly* to the groups and individuals who matter most to your organization.

It does you no good whatsoever to craft a story and then fail to spread it through various methods.

You must find the drama and emotion in your story, and the best way to accomplish that goal is through the three-act format of story-telling. The three-act format focuses on the two critical elements of every compelling story:

- the characters
- the conflict the characters encounter

Here is the three-act format:

Act 1: Introduction of characters and conflict
Act 2: The varied attempts by the characters to resolve the conflict
Act 3: The heroic resolution of the conflict by the lead character

In the classic action thriller *Die Hard*, we meet a New York detective played by Bruce Willis, as he arrives in Los Angeles to celebrate Christmas with his wife. We learn he is also there to attempt to save their estranged marriage, because he truly loves her. Meanwhile, during the office Christmas party, the wife and her coworkers are taken hostage by a group of terrorists.

This is a classic Act 1: the audience meets characters with whom they can relate, and we are introduced to a dire conflict they must resolve.

Act 2 consists of all the varied efforts that Bruce Willis makes to free his beloved wife and resolve their crisis. If you've seen the movie, you'll remember the thrilling attempts to attract the attention of the police and subdue the terrorists, and Willis's challenge to simply stay alive.

(Spoiler alert: if you haven't seen *Die Hard*, the following paragraph will reveal the ending of the original film. I'm compelled to mention this because of my previous experience as a movie reviewer.)

When I first saw *Die Hard* in a theater, the scene where Willis gets the best of the evil mastermind played by Alan Rickman was met by wild applause from the audience. However, the thrill ride was not yet over.

> *A story you keep to yourself has the same value as no story at all.*

When an additional exciting moment ended the film—the kindly police officer who has been communicating by radio throughout the movie with Willis takes out the remaining bad guy—the crowd went berserk again. Act 3 of this movie is a textbook example of a "heroic resolution" that is compelling to the audience.

Notice the result of *Die Hard*'s superb execution of this approach: stellar box office business, for not only the original but also the sequels that followed over the years, not to mention millions of dollars in sales of home video and licensed products.

The impact of the initial *Die Hard*'s success continues to this day. Fox Studios' fifth installment of the adventures of John McClane, *A Good Day to Die Hard*, was given a scheduled release date almost twenty-five years after the original film hit the theaters. Compelling stories and interesting characters can keep an audience interested for many years.

Let's examine how you might use the same three-act formula to create similar success for yourself and your organization.

Act 1

Introduce your story by revealing characters your audience will find engaging and interesting. And as writers since the beginning of communication have recognized, the best way to connect us with characters is to place them in a conflict.

The clash can be as dramatic as 24's Jack Bauer being called upon by CTU to single-handedly save the world in the TV series that ran from 2001 to 2010 or as intimate as a father trying to make his life better for himself and his son in Will Smith's 2006 movie *The Pursuit of Happyness*. It can take as long to resolve as *War and Peace* or can quickly come to a close with a whiter load of laundry in a thirty-second Tide commercial. Without the introduction of characters that we care about and a conflict the audience desires to see resolved, what remains of a story has diminished impact.

Many businesses have been founded because a single entrepreneur fervently desired a better product, or a better life. Yet for some mystical reason, most do not feel that their struggles and challenges merit conveyance to customers and colleagues. So they just muddle along, undifferentiated and merely getting by.

Here's how you begin to discover your story:

Start with a blank sheet of paper—we will call this your "story sheet"—and ask yourself, What conflict did I desire to resolve when I started my business? Or what challenge did the founders of the company seek to conquer when they began it?

If that's too daunting, ponder a favorite client and describe the difficulties he or she encountered prior to engaging your products and services. Somewhere inside, there is a significant (at least to you) conflict that was begging for resolution.

Write it down.

Don't jump too quickly away from this point. Drill deeply into the conflict before proceeding to the next step.

Remember, if your audience fails to be engaged by Act 1, they won't *care* what happens in Acts 2 and 3.

Act 2

Now that you have defined the conflict, describe the pursuit of an answer to the problem. In the real world, as well as in fiction, few of us arrive at the remedy on our first attempt.

(A fictional account where the primary character succeeds from the beginning is both a very *short* and a very *boring* story!)

Describe the varied efforts by your characters to resolve the challenges they faced and the failures they encountered along the way.

For example, to say, "Jane was smart and got an A+ in class," is not a great story.

But to vividly describe Jane as growing up in a poor family that had no high school graduates . . . and her need for superior grades to gain admission to college as well as her necessity for scholarships to pay for her education . . . perhaps without the support and understanding of some of her family . . . as well as her extraordinary efforts to know the material . . . makes the conclusion "Jane got an A+ in class" a much more compelling narrative.

Notice that the results she generated are *identical* in the two presentations.

However, adding her efforts, challenges, and situations to the mix— *in other words, by creating an Act 2*—makes the story of Jane's A+ infinitely more compelling.

To use a business model, you could say, "Tom runs a dry cleaners."

Or you could point out that Tom, faced with new competition and challenges with environmental regulations, became a serious student first—and then a leading proponent of alternative cleaning methods. You could describe that he courageously changed the way his parents and grandparents ran the family business. Tom now creatively manages the dry cleaning establishment in a manner that serves his customers, while also becoming a public example of a "green" business.

Note that in both cases, Tom runs a dry cleaners. When you relate a story with an engaging and interesting Act 2, you now present potential customers with a compelling reason to do business with Tom.

To advance your story, you should begin to isolate numerous aspects that detail the search for resolution you (or your organization's founders) explored or that your customers are currently seeking so you can enhance the impact of your narrative.

Next, write each of these potential facets of your story that you have identified in detail on your "story sheet."

This can effectively be a voluminous quest, as authors such as Tom Clancy and John Grisham seem to prove with every new book, or it can be as concise a pursuit as changing from your current detergent to a new one in a half-minute television commercial.

My experience has always been that it is better to start with more examples than you require and then scale your story down, so you can streamline your efforts for maximum impact.

Act 3

We have now arrived at the conclusion of your story; a compelling Act 3 and your opportunity to become heroic. However, in order to maximize the impact of this act, you must take steps to determine the manner in which your audience prefers your story to conclude.

I was conducting a consulting session with a team of financial advisers when their experience drove this point home to me. "Scott," the principal of the team told me, "we have always prided ourselves on results and returns that beat the market. And we thought we were doing a pretty good job of telling our clients and prospects that we were doing just that. However, for some reason, we were not getting our messages to have the kind of traction that delivers more of the type of high-net-worth prospects any practice desires.

"We would constantly tell them that we were getting higher returns than the market, or than our competition," he continued, "but it didn't seem to make a difference."

What would be the Act 3 for *your* narrative?

Consider several wrap-ups to your story, and write them on your "story sheet."

Then prepare for a vital step in the process.

Screen-Test Your Story

That financial adviser needed to discover something the movie studios have known for decades: you have to screen-test your story, especially when you are evaluating your Act 3.

A CNN report from 1998 relates some big changes in major films as a result of the input of audiences at screenings prior to public release.

For example, Rupert Everett was to have a small role in Julia Roberts's film *My Best Friend's Wedding*—until the screenings clearly showed that audiences wanted much more of him in the movie. "So the ending was scrapped, the set rebuilt, and Everett's character came back for one final appearance," says the network.[7]

In the now classic movie *Fatal Attraction*, screening audiences so intensely despised Glenn Close's character that the ending was rewritten and she was killed off in a revised—and much more gripping—conclusion. (As we look back at them, Act 3 in each of these films is so satisfying to the audience, it is hard to imagine the filmmakers could have considered any other endings.)

If the professional storytellers making multi-million-dollar films have to consider the customer to craft the best ending for their stories, you should not hesitate in seeking your customers' input on yours.

How does this process work for filmmakers? "First, test audiences are recruited from movie lines," CNN reports. "The audience sees the film for free. Afterward, each participant fills out a survey."

This survey asks for opinions similar to those you should seek from customers:

- What you thought of the story
- What five things you liked best
- What five things you liked least
- Which part of the story you liked the most
- Which characters you identified with

CNN continues, "Some members of the audience are asked to join a smaller discussion, known as a focus group. There the process works basically the same way. 'There was a facilitator,' says Robert Kessler of a focus group he attended. 'And he basically asked people to comment on whether they liked or disliked certain characters, whether you thought certain things should have been more developed, less developed, et cetera.'"

The reason this approach is so important is best summarized by acclaimed director Ron Howard, who stated for CNN, "What I would hate to do is put the movie out there, find out that the audience is confused about something or upset about something that you could have fixed, and go, 'I had no idea they'd respond that way.'"[8]

Yet, as our earlier example demonstrates, many of us in business communicate without really understanding how our audience will respond. After the financial adviser screen-tested his Act 3, he reported a different reaction.

"We asked a select few of our 'A' clients what was the most important result of our work for them," he told me. "Not one single client mentioned that we 'beat the market' or 'beat the competition.' It was that they got to go to the Vatican, sail on a dream cruise, or buy a second home in a vacation paradise. We realized that what we were currently promoting was a pretty important Act 3 for *us,* but it wasn't the heroic resolution that *our audience* desired!"

By changing the conclusion of their story to the Act 3 the audience desired—and, it's important to note, one that was totally honest and ethical, as well as meeting their highly regulated industry's standards for compliance—their referrals have grown and their business has improved.

The Next Phase for the Differentiation of High Point University

Imagine now that High Point University must create a compelling story to communicate its clear and creative points of distinction. How would you do it?

Here is the answer: it would all depend upon the audience.

A prospective student would prefer a narrative about a young adult facing the pressures of academic performance combined with the desire for an enjoyable college experience.

A potential donor might wish to be enthralled by a chronicle of a corporate leader facing tremendous challenges in finding highly prepared professionals, who discovers his workforce has become more productive because of the students and graduates of HPU.

The previously mentioned 2012 article from *Bloomberg Businessweek* relates one of the university president's stories to parents:

> Moving to the edge of the stage, [Nido Qubein] picks up a
> bag of Hershey's Kisses and a box of Godiva chocolates. The
> Hershey candy cost about $4, he informs the audience; the
> Godiva, $40. "Both are good," he says, "but only one resides
> in the extraordinary. It presents itself in a way that people find
> compellingly good."

He leans toward the audience, the Godiva box in the palm of his right hand. "Isn't that what you want for your child?"

Obviously, what one finds moving will leave another cold. This should not come as a surprise. Some of the movies my wife hates are my favorites and vice versa. This, of course, is why we can pick up each day's newspaper and discover a varied selection of movies playing to various target audiences. You must customize your story to fit the audience segment you are attempting to attract.

As a Part of Distinction . . .

The old adage "Build a better mousetrap and the world will beat a path to your door" is horribly incorrect and totally out of date. If the planet is unaware of your advantages and cannot Google the path to your doorway, no one will ever arrive to obtain your product.

(Besides that, what customer "beats a path" to anyone's doorway? Just ship it to me overnight.)

If, however, you have developed *clarity* about who and what you are . . . and *creativity* that generates space between you and your competitors . . . and if you have *communicated* those results through a compelling story tailored for the precise audiences you desire to attract . . . you have made major strides in developing the kind of distinction all organizations and professionals covet.

Yet there is one remaining cornerstone. And it is the one that can propel you and your company to greater heights than perhaps you ever imagined.

Executive Summary

I.   The third of the Four Cornerstones of Distinction is *communication*.

A. An organization holding a meeting puts up a sign: "Sales cure everything!"

B. Wrong! Sales may ease the symptoms of a current situation or keep you on life support.

C. Sales, perhaps, *extend* everything. Sales do *not* cure what ails your organization.

D. *Distinction* is the strategy that takes an ailing organization or career and gets you on your feet and back into the race.

    1. Distinction cannot be built for an organization or individual that cannot communicate.

II. A culture of "story junkies"

A. We are a culture that loves to hear and respond to compelling stories.

    1. We are enthralled by the stories of organizations of distinction, from Southwest's founding on a napkin to Apple's start in a garage.

    2. The problem is that we often fail to tell our own stories.

        a. "We're all just cavemen with briefcases, hungry for a wise person to tell us stories."

B. When I returned to my small hometown to speak to the faculty of my school, my third-grade teacher's insight was powerful.

    1. While I had learned my ABCs from the disciplined rote and repetition taught by my mother and grandmother, today students learn their alphabet from Big Bird and Bert and Ernie of *Sesame Street*.

    2. My former teacher concluded, they "expect to be entertained as they are educated."

C. Powerful results follow when customers know your story and find it compelling.

    1. Apple has practically no corporate sales staff, yet some

businesses reported to *Businessweek* that up to 25 percent of their employees are asking to use Macs.

    a. All without a single sales call from Apple.

    b. All driven by customers who know the story.

III. The three-act format of storytelling

    A. Inspired by Joseph Campbell's work, the three-act approach draws drama and emotion from your story.

        1. The approach includes two critical elements:

           a. Characters: the people who inhabit your story and with whom the audience identifies.

           b. Conflict: the challenges these people encounter.

    B. Act 1: Introduction of characters and conflict

        1. Just like Jack Bauer of *24* being called to save the country or John McClane in *Die Hard* trying to save his wife from being taken captive, a powerful story places characters in a situation that creates a dilemma.

        2. It can be as simple as a mother wanting a whiter load of laundry in a thirty-second television commercial.

           a. What conflict does your customer seek to resolve through your product or service?

           b. What challenges were facing your founders when they started your organization?

    C. Act 2: The varied attempts by the characters to resolve the conflict

        1. Act 2 is always the longest of the three acts.

        2. Few of us find remedy in our first attempt.

           a. Therefore, the audience also identifies with our struggle for solution.

        3. Recall all of the approaches taken by Bruce Willis's character to settle his situation in *Die Hard*.

    4. Isolate and detail the numerous aspects that your customers or founders (or you) explored to enhance the impact of your narrative.

  D. Act 3: The heroic resolution of the conflict by the characters

    1. Create a highly compelling conclusion that moves your audience to respond emotionally.

      a. You need to "screen-test" your story—especially your Act 3—with test groups to ensure you are eliciting the maximum impact possible.

IV. The power of story in communication at High Point University

  A. HPU discovered that a story needed to be created for each of their distinctive audiences.

    1. A donor might be moved by the story of HPU alumni developing successful careers, impacting the industry she cared most about.

    2. Prospective students would be more compelled to attend via a story about young adults facing the pressures of academic performance, combined with the desire for an enjoyable experience.

  B. *Every* organization and *each* professional must craft multiple stories targeted to specific audiences.

V. "Build a better mousetrap" isn't true anymore!

  A. The cliché is horrible, incorrect, and totally out of date.

  B. If the world is unaware of your product—and doesn't know how to get to your door—no one will ever arrive to obtain what you are offering.

  C. If, however, you have taken your clarity and creativity and communicated those differentiated aspects through a compelling story, you have made major strides in creating distinction.

Action Steps, Questions, and Ideas

- ♦ Begin your story sheet. Ask yourself, What conflict did I desire to resolve when I began my business career? Or what challenge did the founders of the company seek to overcome when they started their business?

- ♦ On your story sheet, list several of the various attempts that either you or your organization's leaders tried in order to solve the conflict you initially indicated.

- ♦ What is the heroic resolution of your conflict?

- ♦ Write four specific ways you will screen-test your story.

- ♦ How have you varied your story to meet the unique needs of your different audiences?

EIGHT

THE FOURTH CORNERSTONE:
CUSTOMER-EXPERIENCE FOCUS

Middle seat, middle of the night.

On one side of me, next to the window, is a guy I am guessing is the latest parolee from my home state's reformatory. Squeezed into the aisle seat in my row is a man who must be a sumo-wrestling champion. Sandwiched between these two strangers, I'm doing my best at faking sleep, reading a little, sipping a Diet Coke, and fighting claustrophobia. My fellow passengers seem tired and cranky, and so do the flight attendants. Even when the crew can summon the energy to muster a semblance of a smile, their eyes are simultaneously sending subversive signals.

"Shark eyes, man, *shark eyes* . . . ," the guy on the window says to me.

"Uh . . . what? I'm sorry," I reply, thinking I've missed something, "what did you say?"

"Look at 'er," he orders. "She's cold, man. She has shark eyes. Don't want to cross her—she'd probably throw you off this thing."

"In midair!" Mr. Sumo inserts into the conversation—then laughs heartily at his attempt at humor. "She wouldn't give you a drink—or a parachute—on the way out, either!" He guffaws again at his own jokes.

Good grief. *How much longer is it to my destination?*

I'm occupying space between these two because I'm heading to the northern Florida city of Jacksonville to make a presentation to a group of Merrill Lynch executives on the importance of great client service. However, at this moment, I am certainly not on the receiving end of the type of customer-experience focus I strongly recommend that every organization deliver to its clients.

The flight is a couple of hours late—meaning I won't arrive in Jacksonville until a few minutes after midnight, and I'm booked for an early-morning breakfast prior to my speech tomorrow. I'm already counting the few hours I will be able to sleep, knowing I have to be at my very best for the audience.

It's easy to tell this is just another segment in a long day of flights for the crew. Get the cattle . . . uh, *passengers* . . . on the plane, shovel a drink and peanuts their way, hope they keep their mouths shut until landing, get them off the plane, then repeat the process. We are undoubtedly riding on their last flight of the day, and as soon as they can get rid of us, their work is done. From their demeanor, it would seem this cannot happen a moment too soon.

Mr. Sumo evidently swallows a peanut incorrectly and starts to cough. Between hacks, he smiles at the parolee and me and says, "I'm OK . . . just a little too much salt!" Thankful I would not have to attempt to perform the Heimlich maneuver on this man-mountain, I watched as he pressed the call button for the flight attendant.

Slowly approaching the passenger, she stares at him coldly as he asks for a cup of water to relieve his coughing. Acting like a small child, she rolls her eyes to the ceiling, exhales loudly, and says with a tone of disgust, "Just a moment."

About five minutes later, she approaches with a cup of water, pushes it in Mr. Sumo's direction, and is gone before he can say, "Thank you."

After what seems to be an eternity, the captain announces we are beginning our descent into Jacksonville. The flight finally reaches the runway, the aircraft is at the assigned gate, and now it is time for me to grab my beat-up carry-on, gather up my tired, old body, and head for the terminal.

Exiting the building, I realize passengers have formed a line for taxis. After my long flight, I am now going to have a substantial wait for a ride to the hotel—not a pleasant development. I take my place at the end of the queue.

Finally, after watching those in front of me get into other taxis that will whisk them to their various destinations, I have arrived at the front of the line. The next cab is *mine*!

Standing there, exhausted and half-asleep, I notice out of the corner of my eye that my cab is approaching. The driver halts his vehicle in front of me—and then, much to my surprise, jumps out of his cab, points his index finger in my direction, and practically shouts at me: "Are you ready for the *best* cab ride of your *life*?"

Sheepishly, I look over each of my shoulders to see if he's speaking to someone else. When I realize the comment was directed at me, I shrug and say, "Uh . . . well . . . um . . . yeah. I guess so?"

He breaks into a broad smile and says, "Well—*hop on in*!"

Simultaneously, he jogs over to me, grabs my suitcase, and pops open the trunk of his cab as I climb into the backseat. He closes the trunk lid, jumps into the driver's seat, spins around toward me in the back, thrusts out his hand, and inquires, "Mr. McKain?"

Stunned, I respond, "Yes—but how did you know my name?"

Again, he smiles. "Saw it on the name tag on your suitcase. Thought I might as well use it!" Wiggling his hand a bit to reinforce he's waiting on a handshake, he states, "I'm Taxi Terry!"

In my fatigue, all I can think to myself is, "Great. I'm stuck with the motivational cab driver."

"Where we heading tonight, Mr. McKain?" he asks.

"The Marriott downtown," I reply.

"Great!" he exclaims, "Let's check out the weather!"

Weather? It hasn't even crossed my mind at midnight to be concerned about what tomorrow's weather is going to be. Then Taxi Terry touches the dashboard of his cab and a portion of it illuminates. Embedded in the dash is a PDA with a magnifying glass over the screen, meaning I can clearly read it from the backseat. He has directed it to Weather.com for Jacksonville—and I can clearly see the seconds ticking off—meaning I now have the up-to-the-minute weather forecast for my visit.

"I hope you play golf, Mr. McKain," he says, "because you are going to have a beautiful stay in Jacksonville! Tell me, sir," he continues, "if you don't mind my asking, why are you here?"

"I'm in town to give a speech at the hotel to a group of professionals about customer service," I respond.

"*Customer service!*" he exclaims. "I am so *into* that!"

"No kidding," I think.

Then he confounds my expectations once again. He asks, "Would you mind if I record our conversation?" He starts reaching up toward his sun visor.

Meanwhile, I'm thinking, "Who *is* this guy?"

I have to ask the question. "Wait a second," I say. "Why are you equipped to record the conversations that take place in your cab?"

"Well, you see, Mr. McKain," he responds slowly, "let's say Dr. Smith—he's a local customer—gets into my cab for a ride to the airport. And during our conversation he mentions that his daughter, Jill, has just enrolled at Vanderbilt University. As soon as he exits the cab, I hit the button and record that information."

Then more amazing information from Taxi Terry: "Every night when I return home, I take the information from these recordings I have made and enter it into my database. The next time Dr. Smith makes a reservation, this information pops up on my computer. So the doctor gets into the cab, and I ask him, 'By the way, sir, how is Jill doing at Vanderbilt?'"

Terry smiles and asks, "After that, do you think he will ever ride with anyone else?"

In the darkened backseat, I shake my head and think to myself, "No. That doctor will never call anyone else for a trip to the airport!"

During our ride, Taxi Terry educates me on some of his other approaches to the customer experience, but he still has another surprise in store for me. In just about every other cab ride I have experienced on a business trip, upon arrival at the destination the driver presents the passenger with two forms—sometimes printed on opposite sides of the same card, occasionally on separate sheets. One is a receipt the rider can file for expense reimbursement or a tax deduction; the second is a business card, in the hope that the passenger will request the same driver for a return trip once his meeting is near its conclusion.

On this extraordinary trip, however, Taxi Terry pulled up in front of the hotel, ran to the trunk of his car, removed my bag, and held it as if I were a family member. He gently handed the bag to a waiting bellman and proudly announced he was "presenting Mr. McKain and his luggage!"

Then he turned to me without a card or paper or form in his hand and said, "Mr. McKain, I realize you are going to need a receipt to document the trip for your business purposes. And someone brought you here, so someone is going to have to take you back to the airport—and I hope that's *me*! You can print your receipt and schedule your return trip on my website at www.TaxiTerry.com."

He was not finished! "One more thing, Mr. McKain?" he requested. "You mentioned you fly a great deal . . . which probably means you are riding in a lot of cabs. Well, I'm franchising these ideas. So if you ever run into a cab driver who could use some assistance with customer service"—I am thinking that would probably be approximately *all of them*—"then you just tell them about Taxi Terry!"

I wanted to give him a standing ovation on the spot. It was a perfect example of the ultimate in a customer-experience focus.

Where Else Would You Look?

Comedian Jeff Foxworthy was joking about phrases we all utter without thinking. I laughed out loud when he mentioned that people hunting for a lost item often absent-mindedly announce, "I found it in the last place I looked!"

Well, of course you did! Once you came across it, why would you continue searching?

I feel that way when I'm asked about whether an organization should have a "customer-experience" focus. I'm always thinking, "Well, where *else* could you focus? And why would you keep on searching?"

Think about it for a moment: is it productive to focus internally, on the politics and structure of an organization? Obviously those areas require consideration, examination, and care. But if that's your primary area of concentration, your attention is in the wrong place.

The same is true if your organization's focal point is on the market and your share price. We know, from a historical perspective, that organizations that are differentiated from their competition and distinct in the marketplace are the winners over the long haul. However, we also recognize that the market often tends to reward incremental, short-term gains when these are viewed through the lens of daily trading. If you're centered primarily upon what your shares are doing at this moment, or just for this quarter, you may be missing long-term opportunities.

The purpose of this chapter is to demonstrate why the focus of you and your organization should be squarely on the experience you are creating for your customers.

It will also illustrate the fundamental difference between *customer service* and the *customer experience* and present the five specific steps you must take to create the Ultimate Customer Experience®. In addition, the chapter will explain why those organizations claiming to have a "value added" program are probably not providing their customers with nearly enough value.

What's It All About?

Over the years, we have all heard the standard definitions for the "purpose of business":

- "The purpose of business is to make a profit."
- "The purpose of business is to obtain and retain customers profitably."
- Legendary management guru Peter Drucker said, "There is only one valid definition of business purpose: to create a customer."

My meager attempt from my first book was simply this:

- The purpose of any business is to profitably create experiences so compelling to customers that their loyalty to your organization becomes assured.

If you drill deep into that definition, you'll discover it means a *customer-experience focus* is primary.

Your ability to profitably deliver upon that effort will determine the success and the distinction of both your organization and you as a professional.

The Definition of Customer Focus

When your efforts and your organization's actions are wrapped up in "profitably creating experiences so compelling loyalty is assured," you have reached the point that this cornerstone advocates. It is the echelon where the customer's experience is at the center of every decision the organization makes at all levels of the organization.

This characterization gets to the heart of the difference between the culture of "customers are the foundation of *who we are*" as opposed to the approach of "customer service is a part of *what we have to do.*"

Customers realize that "what you do" can easily change with economic fads or organizational whims. They know "who you are" is the basic expression of what you stand for and what you will continue to be. It is the embodiment of the old adage "Actions speak louder than words."

It means that centering our focus upon the customer experience is a decision we have made about how we are going to exist . . . now and forever.

Focus on creating distinctive experiences for your clients and prospects.

Customer focus cannot become just a short-term method we are executing because our competition is doing so (which is exactly the approach many organizations take, and which was described earlier as one of the Three Destroyers of Differentiation).

The blog Customers Are Always offers its definition of a customer-focused strategy as "a plan that emphasizes the needs of a particular customer segment over that of the organization."[1] And Maria Palma posted a nice addition to this concept on the blog when she wrote, "A strategy is not 'customer-focused' when a company is obsessed with the numbers and has the scarcity mentality. Instead of asking themselves, 'Is this for the greater good of our customers?', they're constantly asking, 'Did we make our sales goals?'"[2]

To create a compelling differentiation in today's market, it's not enough for organizations and professionals of distinction to implement a "customer-focused" strategy. Remember, our cornerstone states: Distinction is created by developing a *customer-experience* focus. In other words, concentrating on customers is not enough if you want to become a true market leader. You must follow Taxi Terry's example and take it to an even higher level and focus on the creation of distinctive *experiences* for your clients and prospects.

Aren't Service and Experience the Same?

My work exposes me to many individuals and organizations that have yet to explore the fundamental difference between providing customer service and creating a customer experience.

This often occurs because there are three separate and distinct levels of customer interaction. For an organization to excel, it must examine each of these levels as unique and create a plan to strategically improve performance at every level.

Level One—Processing: the basic elements of the transaction; the aspects that the customer has a right to expect you to deliver upon because they have chosen to spend money with you and your organization.

Level Two—Service: the steps you and your organization will undertake to make processing more efficient, palatable, enjoyable, and/ or friendly to your customers to enhance the likelihood they will repeat their business.

Level Three—Experience: the commitment, as well as the actual execution of specific strategies, required to create the element of emotion. This results in an intensely personal connection for customers.

It is only at this point that loyalty from the client toward your organization (or you) is generated.

Progressive Attainment of Success

The attainment of these levels is progressive. If you fail in terms of processing—for example, if the food at your restaurant isn't properly prepared or if I had to wait an extended period after the time for which I had reserved my table—then the higher levels of interaction have little traction.

If my flight is three hours late arriving at O'Hare, I really don't care how hot the coffee was that the flight attendants served. However, when the flight's on time and uneventful, then receiving a nice cup of java enhances my evaluation of your airline's ability to provide me with what I want.

This morning, I went into our local Starbucks to pick up my wife Tammy's favorite morning beverage. I think it's a pretty complicated concoction. She wants an iced mocha, skim milk, with an extra shot of espresso, and just a light touch of whipped cream on top.

This morning's drink was prepared perfectly (level one: processing). The line in the Starbucks moved quickly, and the place is a clean and inviting environment (level two: service). When I approached the counter, I was greeted with, "Good morning, Mr. McKain! How's the book coming along?" (Well, you can imagine that when you are working hard to complete a manuscript, it's a pretty emotional thing to have someone concerned!)

And at the point where the barista behind the machine asked, "Picking up the usual drink for Tammy?" I had absolutely reached the point of *experience*. All I had to do was ask for Tammy's "usual," and the barista knew the formula for her favorite drink.

That's not just a customer-*service* focus—it's a customer-*experience* focus.

As I'm writing this, I realize I don't know if the iced mochas are more or less expensive at Starbucks than at McDonald's or other coffee shops serving a similar drink. I assume Starbucks probably charges a price that's a little bit higher. However, here's the critical point: *my experience makes price irrelevant.*

Creating a Customer-Experience Focus from the Top

If you are in a position of significant leadership at your organization, the creation of the customer-experience focus begins with your vision.

* Are you willing to seek what is now commonly called the "voice of the customer"?
* Do you have feedback systems in place that will provide you with unaltered evaluations from your clients?
* Perhaps most important, are you willing to ask at every juncture how each action of your company will impact customers and create more compelling differentiation for your organization?

Currently, I'm dealing with an organization that has had a transition in leadership. The new CEO is completely committed to changing the culture of the organization and putting a stake in the ground that his leadership legacy will be one of a concerted and disciplined focus on the client experience.

The challenge is, many of his managers believe this is a "nice" approach, but they want to delegate the effort of customer experiences to a single client-services department.

One manager even intimated to me that he wanted the "client-facing people to take care of the customers so I can just do my job." (I'm convinced that if this manager truly believes customers in today's marketplace are somebody else's job, then he should be out of a job!)

If you are unsuccessful in creating distinction in the marketplace through the Four Cornerstones—and particularly through this one—then it practically becomes ensured that a mediocre voyage on the sea of sameness is the *best* you'll be able to achieve. Please understand, too, that abject failure is a definite possibility.

I admire the new CEO, but my esteem is slight compared to the manner in which his colleagues will respect and appreciate him in a few years. He not only has an opportunity to lead an organization; he is taking advantage of an opportunity to pioneer a new level of client connectivity and distinction in his industry.

If you are the leader of a company—regardless of its size—do you have similar courage and commitment?

Creating a Customer-Experience Focus from Elsewhere

But what if you're not the person in charge? How can you create this point of distinction for yourself?

The answer is not an easy one. However, in all honesty, it is the only one available: you have to just *do it*, anyway.

You must examine your specific area of corporate responsibility and become the CEO of your own customer-experience-focused mini-firm within the organization.

If your management imitates an ostrich and puts its organizational head in the sand during these times of economic volatility, you have to take the initiative and responsibility to do all *you* can do for your customers—and yourself—by personally employing these customer-focused distinction strategies.

If you are successful in this effort, you may very well find that one (or more) of these five circumstances occurs:

1. Your success moves you to a higher level of responsibility within your organization.
2. Your distinction attracts the attention of a competitor with the proper vision and strategy.
3. You outlast the current management team, and your achievements and client connectivity make you highly desirable to a new regime.

4. One of your customers realizes you would be an enormous asset on his or her team, and offers you a position with his organization.

5. You discover you would like to be the captain of your own ship, and you become an entrepreneur.

Yet, as corny as it sounds, these should be residual reasons for creating a compelling experience for your clients or customers.

The fundamental reason to execute this strategy is that it's *purely the right thing to do.*

The right thing to do is executing for your customers the very connection you desire when you are the client. It is becoming the living embodiment of the "golden rule" we have likely been encouraged to live by, regardless of the specific cultural or religious tradition in which we were raised. Cultures everywhere in the world acknowledge the wisdom of this rule.

- Hindus learn in Mahabharata 5:1517, "This is the sum of duty: do not do to others what would cause pain if done to you."
- Islam teaches in Number 13 of Imam Al-Nawawi's Forty Hadiths: "None of you [truly] believes until he wishes for his brother what he wishes for himself."
- Followers of Confucianism learn in Analects 15:23, "Do not do to others what you do not want them to do to you."[3]
- As a Christian, I believe the words of the Holy Bible in Luke 6:31, "As ye would that men should do to you, do ye also to them likewise."

In addition, my friend and colleague Dr. Tony Alessandra lectures on "The Platinum Rule," which is: "Do unto others the way *they* want to be done unto."

Regardless of your individual beliefs, it is almost impossible to imagine a detrimental outcome from executing strategies placing customers at the center of every action you and your organization undertake.

Creating the Ultimate Customer Experience

To attain this focus, you need to create what I have been calling (for more than two decades) the Ultimate Customer Experience® (UCE). You can find a detailed examination of the UCE in my book *Expand Distinction: ALL Business Is Show Business.*

However, for our purposes to create distinction, here's a brief, five-step look at how you can produce and implement the UCE for your organization:

Step One: Ask a Question

The first step to create the Ultimate Customer Experience is to take a legal pad and (individually or with your team) ask this question: "What would happen if everything went exactly right?"

Then record all of the responses.

Doing this is more complex than it might first appear. For example, if everything went exactly right:

* How many times would the phone ring before it was answered?
    * What percentage of your calls should be fielded by a live person instead of via technology?
* What sensations would be experienced by customers when they walk into your store?
    * What would the temperature be?
    * What would customers hear?
    * In other words, what should the store sound like?

The single-most important factor here is to keep drilling down to the smallest aspects of your interactions with customers and prospects. Constantly push for what would have to happen for that contact to be *exactly right*.

For example, I've heard Starbucks does not allow its associates to wear cologne or perfume on the days they work. The reason is obvious. When you walk into the coffee shop, Starbucks wants you to savor the aroma of the coffee, not wonder if you are inhaling Chanel No. 5 or Calvin Klein's Obsession.

You must examine your interaction with your customers and prospects with extraordinary precision in order to get it exactly right. That's the standard of the Ultimate Customer Experience.

Step Two: Engage Your Customer in the Process

When there is enhanced interaction, what follows is enhanced connectivity. Therefore, it is imperative that you involve your customers in the process of creating the UCE. (After all, how can it be "ultimate" if it fails to deliver what the customer *really* wants?)

The most basic—and often most powerful—approach to involving the customer is simply to ask, "If you could describe the ultimate experience of doing business with an organization like ours, what would that be?" (Then you *listen!*)

The fundamental challenge so many organizations and professionals experience with this approach to customers is that just listening to them at this point seems counterintuitive.

When a customer presents you with an answer, it gives you an opportunity to initiate a transaction. Therefore, you may find it hard to resist the chance to "close the sale." For example, as your client answers your UCE question, she may state that she seeks something you already provide. Your natural inclination may be to butt in and say, "We do that!"

At this juncture, then, from the customer's perspective, this entire process immediately appears to be nothing more than a sophisticated sales call—not an attempt to improve her customer experience.

And this situation might additionally mean that you (unintentionally) inhibit the relationship. Just as in your personal situations with friends and family, customers desire to be listened to and appreciated. When you attempt to push the customer and close a transaction, you may miss out on hearing highly insightful and revealing information.

Step Three: Sync the Information

Next, match the steps you have internally developed to create the UCE with the hopes and dreams that have been expressed through this process by your customers.

In some areas, the two may fit together quite nicely—in other words, what the customers told you *they* wanted in the UCE, and what *you* outlined through the process, may turn out to be highly similar.

However, I have also found some outcomes to be highly conflicting. If this is the case, realize that you are creating the UCE to engage customers! You must give them the benefit of the doubt.

On the other hand, you've got to temper this aspect with a point we've previously discussed: sometimes your vision of the future is more enhanced and profound than that of your customers. *Your* insight is required to build the UCE, as well.

Step Four: Outline the Roadblocks

Another question is vital to the development of the UCE: "What roadblocks prevent us from executing the UCE for every customer or prospect at every point of interaction?"

- Make a list of as many barriers as you can.
- Next, investigate and analyze each of them.

Some will be outdated corporate policies, while others will be misguided strategies. All of these UCE obstructions should be intensely scrutinized and, hopefully, eliminated.

Step Five: Execute!

If only it were that simple, right?

Look, I know that none of us—no matter our position within the company, from owner to custodian—can just snap our fingers and put a thorough strategy into action.

Almost always, the Ultimate Customer Experience boils down to a commitment that is made by employees throughout an organization.

A couple of days ago, a United Airlines employee stood behind the ticket kiosk with my driver's license in one hand, my boarding pass in the other, and a computer screen with my reservation in front of her. She was literally surrounded with forms that had my name on them, yet she never used "Scott" or "McKain" at any point in our interaction.

It's impossible to create an experience—much less the UCE—without executing little points of contact properly. The CEO can insist upon it, yet if it is not actually delivered by a frontline employee, the customer often fails to feel as if his or her experience has a customer focus.

However, please consider this: why do you suppose that we constantly read and hear about the same companies all the time? You know the ones: Starbucks, Apple, Southwest, Nordstrom.

I believe the reason is simply because so unbelievably few organizations actually execute on the promise of the Ultimate Customer Experience. That's how breathtakingly difficult it really is. However, the spectacular success of a few organizations should also clearly display how critical it is for all of us to endeavor to deliver the UCE.

A Presidential Campaign's Focus on the "Customer"

Much has been made by the political pundits on the connection Barack Obama established with his supporters throughout his 2008 campaign. Let me give you an individual perspective because, at the end of the day, the customer experience is intensely personal.

First, however, this disclaimer: I did not contribute financially to either of the 2008 presidential candidates, nor did I during the election process of 2012. My vote and support is a private matter. However, I do sign up online so that I can receive the messages sent to supporters on all major candidate's websites. It's a fascinating bit of research everyone can do to study the effort made to convince you—the prospective voter/customer—to choose one option/candidate over another.

Throughout the 2008 campaign, Obama's team was in much more frequent and personal contact with their supporter list than any other candidate was in contact with his or her list. Nothing, though, is a better example than the e-mail I received on the night of the election in November 2008.

While sitting at home and watching CNN on that historic evening, I saw a report stating that President-elect Obama would soon be heading to Grant Park in his hometown of Chicago, Illinois, to speak to the massive throng of supporters gathered to cheer their successful leader. Just then, I heard the tone from my iPhone announcing that I'd just received a new e-mail message. I was astonished to read the following:

Friend—

I'm about to head to Grant Park to talk to everyone gathered there, but I wanted to write to you first.

We just made history. And I don't want you to forget how we did it.

You made history every single day during this campaign—
every day you knocked on doors, made a donation, or talked to
your family, friends, and neighbors about why you believe it's
time for change.

I want to thank all of you who gave your time, talent, and
passion to this campaign.

We have a lot of work to do to get our country back on track,
and I'll be in touch soon about what comes next.

But I want to be very clear about one thing . . . All of this
happened because of you.

Thank you,

Barack

Well, in all honesty, I didn't knock on any doors, or make a donation, or give any time or talent to the campaign. However, the simple
fact that someone—whether Obama himself or the extraordinarily customer experience–focused professionals he had chosen for his team—
first had the insight to think of this, and then execute it at precisely
the right moment, is extraordinarily impressive. It is an epitome of the
Ultimate Customer Experience.

Reexamine the message and notice its perfection in creating an Ultimate Customer Experience. The new president is getting ready to go
speak to several hundred thousand people . . . but *first*, he wanted to
send *me* this e-mail! (Okay, I realize that millions undoubtedly received
this identical message, too. However, that's not what you are thinking
as you're sitting there reading it. It created a personal effect and connection.) And he told me that all of this happened because of me. Finally, the
44th president of the United States signed my message simply "Barack."

Yet when I examine the e-mails and other messages I receive
from companies where I actually *do* spend money, I often find them

oddly impersonal and formal. There is little to no recognition of my importance to the company, even though, as a customer, I and those like me are their lifeblood. Organizations seem to focus on the mailing list more than what the message to that list conveys. They seem to center upon the communication strategy infinitely more than the communication quality.

I'm left to wonder, why is it a company can customize a bill or statement—knowing precisely how much I owe them—yet not care to know anything else about me or about how they can personalize other types of communication as much as they individualize my invoice?

The electronic message I received that night in 2008 from the Obama campaign is a perfect example of how an Ultimate Customer Experience blends both technology and strategy with the intense personalization and heightened emotional connection that customers covet.

However, there is an additional aspect the campaign should have considered that we will discuss in the last chapter of this book.

The Value-Added Approach

We have all observed many organizations that, rather than execute a customer experience–focused approach and deliver UCEs, instead offer "value-added" inducements to their clients and prospects.

Here's my fundamental problem with this strategy: when we do not possess enough of something that we want or need, we desire to *add* to what we have, until we reach a point of satisfaction.

In other words, if the tea isn't sweet enough for me, I'll add sugar or a sugar substitute until it reaches the taste I crave. If you don't have enough savings to provide for your retirement, you'll hopefully make deposits into your account until you reach a satisfactory balance.

Note that the fundamental reason we feel required to augment and increase what we have is that we didn't *already possess* some vital element in the quantity we desired.

So, here are two questions for you:

* When an organization approaches you with a value-added proposition, does that mean the company failed to provide you with enough value in what it had *originally* offered, so now it feels required to bolt on some more?
* When a professional discusses her value add with a prospect, is this approach merely an attempt to recover from an inability to deliver what the customer *really* wanted in the first place?

If you are truly connected to customers, then providing significant and distinct value through your products and services—and assisting clients in growing their own results—should be an integral part of every action. It's not something that has to be added as a separate function.

When you are required to add something to an existing mix, then by definition that element is not a part of the original article or is available in a quantity so limited, the client has become disconnected.

Visionary leaders and insightful organizations focus their attention on their customers in a manner that creates growth and strategic differentiation for their clients. Through that effort, they cannot help gaining both for themselves, as well.

Do You Really Believe . . . ?

Do you think Nordstrom has workshops to teach associates its value-added proposition? I don't. I believe that the customer experience has been woven into the fabric of everything the company does.

Do you believe Steve Jobs gathered his troops together at Apple before the introduction of the iPhone and asked, "Okay, great product. Now what's our value add?"

When he closed every Starbucks for training, did Howard Schultz remind his baristas to "remember the customer's name" because it is a good idea for creating added value? Of course not.

All the elements that create true value for the customer are viewed by these stellar organizations as *intrinsic*. They describe the very essence of what the organization is all about. This means that what distinct organizations deliver cannot be segmented into what is "value added" and what is not.

> *What distinct organizations deliver cannot be easily segmented into what is "value added" and what is not.*

If you say you are a sales organization with a value-added program, your clients will perceive you for exactly what you are—a bunch of sales guys and gals with a product to hawk and a bag of goodies that you'll sprinkle their way if they buy from you. In other words, you are exactly like everyone else who is calling on them.

My belief is that organizations and individuals need to look higher than to a value-added program. We all need to reach for *strategic differentiation*.

In other words, from their very conception, the strategies we are executing as an organization are so focused and provide so much value to the customers that we never find ourselves having to develop and implement a *separate* program to add value. Our differentiation is not an add-on or option because true distinction is always essential to who we are.

My experience, however, has been that many organizations view the customer as just one of the facets they must deal with to build a successful business, instead of as their very reason for existence. Numerous professionals may give lip service to customers as the chief priority. However, when you examine how the organizations actually spend their time, it becomes apparent that they value other aspects as infinitely more essential.

I have a considerable disagreement with a sales executive (whom I tremendously respect on a personal level) at a company where I have done a significant amount of work. He states, "We are primarily a sales organization. Our 'value add' enhances our access to customers and prospects and elevates our visibility in the marketplace. However, if someone on our team is hitting his or her numbers without using our value-add program, then it's an optional resource for that person."

Here's the reason for my resistance to this line of thinking: do you think Nordstrom managers would ever, in a million years, say to the sales team, "Look, if you are hitting your numbers in women's shoe sales, you can sell them any way you want"?

There is *zero* chance they would ever take that approach. Nordstrom would teach that its way of creating the experience and dealing with customers is just "how it's done." It is certainly not optional in any manner whatsoever.

Les Schwab Tires would never, ever suggest, "You know, if your store is moving enough tires to make your goals, just walk to the cars. In fact, why not let customers come up to the counter just like our competitors do? Running is optional if your store is hitting its numbers."

High Point University would never be the same if President Qubein announced at a faculty and staff meeting, "Admissions and endowment goals have been exceeded, so don't worry about that 'inspiring environment' stuff anymore. Just do your jobs." In fact, Qubein would be the first to emphasize to his team that creating the inspiring environment *is* their job—it is just the way things are done at HPU.

It All Comes Together . . .

Notice how all of the Cornerstones of Distinction are coming together?

The company that will not develop clarity will find it enormously difficult to execute a strategy of customer-experience focus. If you haven't defined who and what you really are, it becomes impossible to deliver experiences to customers that are congruent with your organization's focus. (This is obvious, because you don't *have* a focus.) If you failed to be creative and are therefore unsuccessful at communicating any points of distinction you've created, then the expectations of the prospect or customer aren't in alignment with a customer-experience focus.

However, let's reverse the outlook to one that is positive.

- If you are clear about what you stand for, you can develop the precision necessary to deliver to customers the compelling experiences that ensure loyalty.
- You can communicate your individual and organizational distinction, in part because you're focused on customers and because your actions are aligned. You truly "practice what you preach."
- The customer-experience focus is the right place for you to concentrate your efforts.

Center your efforts on strategic differentiation through a customer-experience focus. It is the final piece in the puzzle to build distinction as you differentiate yourself from your competition.

There You Have It

The Four Cornerstones of Distinction are now in place, and you can begin to build an organization that is differentiated and a career that is a hallmark of excellence.

Our next chapter will begin to wrap a ribbon around our package, as we build upon our cornerstones.

Executive Summary

I.   The last of the Four Cornerstones of Distinction is *customer-experience focus.*

A. If you are seeking distinction, where *else* would you look?

    B. Yet many organizations focus internally, on the politics and structure of their company.

        1. That's an important issue; however, if it is your primary area of concentration, your attention is in the wrong place.

            a. What a "business" is all about: The purpose of any business is to profitably create experiences so compelling to its customers that their loyalty becomes assured.

            b. If you drill into that definition, you'll discover it means that inherent in the process of a successful business is a customer-experience focus.

                i. Your ability to deliver upon this effort will determine the success of your organization or your career.

II. Customer-experience focus is who we are!

    A. Distinctive organizations view a focus upon the customer experience as an integral part of who they are.

        1. Non-differentiated companies and professionals view it as "one of the things we have to do."

        2. That difference is subtle yet profound.

    B. A customer-experience focus emphasizes the needs of customers over those of the organization.

        1. You lack a customer-experience focus when you are obsessed with numbers and have a scarcity mentality.

III. Customer service and the customer experience are not the same.

    A. There are three levels at which you interact with your customers: processing, service, and experience.

    B. Success in delivering at one level means the customer allows you the opportunity to advance higher on the scale.

    C. The higher the level of interaction, the more engaged the customer.

        1. Engaged customers become loyal customers.

    D. Level One: Processing

       1. Processing consists of the basic elements of the transaction.

       2. Processing contains what the customer has a right to expect when they choose to do business with you.

    E. Level Two: Service

       1. Service consists of the steps you take to ensure processing is efficient, palatable, and enjoyable for the customer.

       2. Points such as "being friendly" and "answering the phone promptly" fall under service.

    F. Level Three: Experience

       1. The customer experience adds the elements of *personalization* and *emotion*.

       2. When you creatively execute strategies that cause the customer to feel you are offering a solution that is intensely personal to their needs—and when they are emotionally connected to you and your organization—you have created a customer experience.

       3. The customer experience transcends transactions.

       4. The customer experience is where customer loyalty is created.

IV. Creating the customer-experience focus

    A. From the top: CEOs and top managers seeking to create the customer-experience focus should:

       1. Specifically communicate their vision of the experience.

       2. Listen to the "voice of the customer."

       3. Have a feedback system in place that will provide them with unaltered evaluations from their clients.

       4. Ask at every juncture how each action of the company will impact customers and create more compelling experiences.

    B. From elsewhere in the business: If you do not have top leadership with your same vision regarding the customer-experience focus, you need to:

1. Examine your area of personal responsibility and become the CEO of your own "mini-firm" that does have the proper focus within your organization.

2. Take the initiative and the responsibility to do all you can for your customers.

   a. This approach is simply the "right thing to do."

   b. And it will have residual benefit for you and your career that can be substantial and long-lasting.

V. Steps to creating the Ultimate Customer Experience®

   A. Step One: Ask a question.

      1. Ask yourself or your team, "What would happen if *everything* went *exactly* right?"

         a. Record the responses.

         b. This is a more complex exercise than it first appears to be.

         c. Be highly detailed and precise about your answers.

   B. Step Two: Engage your customer in the process.

      1. Ask your customers, "If you could describe the ultimate experience of doing business with an organization like ours, what would that be?"

         a. Record their responses

      2. Listen!

         a. During their descriptions, customers will often point out something that you or your organization is already doing.

         b. This is not a time to be selling or telling. If you start talking about your strong points, the customer now perceives they have been deceived, that this is not a process to serve them better but instead to sell them more.

   C. Step Three: Sync the information.

      1. Match the steps you internally developed to the points your

       customers have identified.

    2. Where these points sync are high-priority items.

  D. Step Four: Outline the roadblocks.

    1. Identify the specific areas where executing these steps will be most difficult for you and your organization.

      a. Some will be outdated policies, others misguided strategies.

      b. Hopefully, all roadblocks will be eliminated.

  E. Step Five: Execute!

    1. Easy to say, infinitely harder to do.

    2. Delivering the Ultimate Customer Experience® depends upon the personal dedication and discipline of every person within the organization.

VI. "Value added" *isn't* "customer experience–focused!"

  A. When an organization says it has a "value added" approach or inducement, what does that really mean?

  B. When we are required to supplement or augment something, it usually means we didn't possess enough of a vital element (in the quantity that we desired) in the first place.

    1. For example, if the tea isn't sweet enough, we add sugar.

    2. If the taste is great we do not feel the need to add anything.

  C. Distinct organizations are so connected to customers that they provide significant value as an integral part of every action.

  D. Value does not have to be added when it is a part of the very fabric of your business.

    1. Nordstrom doesn't add value to the way they sell shoes. It's just the way they do it.

    2. Apple didn't add value to the iPhone. It's just the way they designed and built it.

    3. Starbucks doesn't add value via baristas being friendly and remembering your name. It's just who they are.

    4. High Point University doesn't add value to the student experience. Value is a direct result of the qualities they personify.

  E. When you have strategic differentiation, you are so focused—and provide so much value—there is no need for a separate program or an add-on option.

    1. True distinction is always congruent with who you are.

VII. It all comes together.

  A. Without clarity, how can you have a focus on the customer experience?

  B. Without creativity, how can you deliver compelling communication?

    1. When you are clear about what you stand for, you can develop the precision necessary to deliver to customers the compelling experiences that ensure loyalty.

    2. You can communicate your individual and organizational distinction because you are focused on your customers.

  C. The Four Cornerstones of Distinction—the foundation of an organization or a professional—are now in place. This is a hallmark of excellence.

Action Steps, Questions, and Ideas

- ◆ What would happen if everything went exactly right in terms of the customer experience? Be highly specific in your answers.
- ◆ Write down how you have specifically involved your customers in helping you develop your strategies to enhance relationships. If you haven't already done so, then list the ways that you will get them engaged.
- ◆ What are the roadblocks preventing the UCE?

NINE

MORE LESSONS IN DISTINCTION

It's amazing to me all that has transpired in the years since this book was originally written.

From the growth of the iPhone, the introduction of the iPad, and the passing of Steve Jobs to the proliferation of Facebook, Twitter, and other forms of social media . . . from the rash of home foreclosures and the decline in the housing market, the passing of Obamacare and the Supreme Court decision upholding it, and the fallout of TARP to problems with the Euro, the Occupy Wall Street (and other places, as well) movement, and tsunamis, earthquakes and other astonishing natural disasters . . . it has been an extraordinary period in human history, and in business as well.

Yet it's obvious from the continued success of the vast majority of the organizations discussed in the first edition that the importance of creating distinction has never been more vital than right now. So before we conclude, here are some assorted ideas about distinction gained since my original research and writing that may help paint a more complete picture.

Following Up on an Example

Throughout this book, we've looked at the 2008 presidential campaign of then-Senator Barack Obama as an example of creating distinction. However, his 2012 re-election campaign presents us with an additional aspect of what you can expect to encounter when you create distinction.

In an interview in *Playboy* published in April 2012, *New York Times* columnist David Brooks remarked that he was disappointed with President Obama and with his own decision to vote for Obama in the 2008 election.

Conversely, he also mentioned that his good friend, the *Washington Post's* E. J. Dionne, remained excited by Obama's performance and happy with how he had cast his ballot.

Interestingly—and please remember this is *not* a political discussion; it is about how a customer/voter evaluates your performance—Brooks then explains his reason for dissatisfaction and his friend's justification for the opposite conclusion.

Brooks expected Obama to be a person who would reach across the aisle, work with the Republicans to bring hope and change, bridge the divide between the parties, and find a way to get things done for the country by building consensus.

On the other hand, Dionne (according to Brooks) viewed Obama as the liberal's hope after eight years of George W. Bush. Dionne trusted that Obama would make a stand for the left, get America out of Iraq, make sweeping changes in health care, and assert a more active government to protect the lower and middle class.

Here is the critical issue for you to consider for your business: both of these very smart people created their widely varied perceptions based upon *exactly the same* information.

Obama didn't give one speech to Brooks and another to Dionne. Both journalists studied the same information, watched the same campaign ads, listened to the same speeches, and read the same interviews. (Let's face it, too . . . they probably did a lot more of that than the average American!)

And they still came up with wildly divergent perceptions and polar opposite evaluations of Obama's performance.

Your business, just like the Obama campaign of 2008, can create such compelling messages that it inspires people seeking many different outcomes to choose to vote for (or do business with) you and your organization. That is critically important, and extraordinarily difficult to do.

But here is what's even harder: performing at such a high level that a huge percentage of those who chose you the first time come back for more. It is an example of what makes maintaining distinction in business so darn tough.

A critical question is: are you creating not only a memorable and distinctive story but also one you can *continue to deliver upon*, so your customers maintain their level of commitment to you?

Are You Creating a Distinctive Story?

Since it's not the job of the voter, prospect, customer, or employee to create and develop your story, the question remains: have you done all you can to craft your clear, creative communication to create distinction?

Immediately after I finish a presentation, I'm fortunate to receive comments on implementing the Ultimate Customer Experience and on creating organizational distinction. Give it a month, however, and these same people remember Taxi Terry and our small-town grocery store. Why is that the case?

An article in the May 2012 edition of *Fast Company* provides a great insight into this phenomenon. In an interview, Steve Jobs relates an epiphany he had shortly after he and his kids watched the DVD of *Snow White*. Jobs tells the interviewer, Brent Schlender:

The technology of what we've been laboring on over the past twenty years becomes part of the sedimentary layer. But when *Snow White* was re-released [in 2001], we were one of the 28 million families that went out and bought a copy of it. This was a film that is sixty years old, and my son was watching it and loving it. I don't think anybody's going to be beating on a Macintosh sixty years from now.[1]

As the article states, Jobs recognized that "People remember *stories* more than *products*."

The fundamental question for you is this: why are you spending so much time on the product or service, and practically *none* on the story?

What's the story you have to tell? Your organization . . . your products and services . . . your customers . . . you . . . there is a story about each of these, and chances are you aren't telling it with the power and precision you could.

In the years following the publication of the first edition of this book, executives constantly quizzed me about clarity, creativity, and customer-experience focus. However, only a fraction desire to discuss the importance of communication through the power of story.

That failure to create a compelling story is costing companies both immediate business and long-term customer engagement.

Consider this: if you're having a difficult time developing and refining a story to emotionally connect with colleagues and customers, why not hire a writer to assist you? Seriously. You wouldn't try to perform surgery on yourself; so why would you assume if you have no skills in crafting dramatic, memorable stories that you could do that activity as well as a true pro? If you want a story to be remembered, spend some resources and have it crafted.

In fact, you may be better off if you hire two or three writers, then choose from their efforts. Multiple angles on your stories provide exponentially greater insight into what your customers will consider to be compelling.

As I've learned from my own business, if people can remember your story, they retell it (we call this a *recommendation*) and they want to hear it again (we call this *customer loyalty*). Both are critical to your success.

For some reason, we always ask what we are doing to create a product that customers will *buy*, but we seldom ask what we are doing to provide what people are going to *remember*.

What are you doing today to create a compelling story for your product, company, and yourself that will be repeatable and memorable?

Are You Delivering an Ultimate Customer Experience?

Another area of critical importance is the fourth cornerstone—a customer-experience focus. There are many organizations that will be clear and creative, then, for some unknown reason, deliver a customer experience that pretty much defines mediocrity. However, as I discovered not long ago in Los Angeles, even a business that has received a remarkable amount of publicity can decide not to rest on its laurels and can continue to step up and deliver an Ultimate Customer Experience.

Sure, I have seen the multitude of pictures from the paparazzi of celebrities entering and departing the famed Beverly Hills eatery Spago. It was part of the reason I thought it would be a great place to take my wife to dinner for her birthday.

(This birthday was one of the "big ones," too, if you know what I mean. However, if I tell you *which* one, she may not allow me to celebrate any birthdays with her in the future!)

The timing was perfect: I delivered a speech at Pepperdine University with the legendary George Foreman on Friday, my wife arrived on Friday night, and Saturday was her big day. I made reservations and hoped we would receive a great experience for her important milestone.

As we checked into our hotel, the desk clerk quietly informed me the special birthday plate of desserts I had requested would be arriving from room service later that evening. Naturally, I kept that a secret from my bride, and we left the hotel to stroll Rodeo Drive and window-shop before we headed for our dinner.

Then, only about ninety minutes before our reservation, it occurred to me I had really messed up. I had completely forgotten to inform the restaurant of the special reason for our visit. I quickly called, and they assured me not to worry; my wife would be cared for in a remarkable manner.

When we entered and I stated my name and reservation time, they acted as if we were frequent diners. (This was my third time there in about fifteen years!) Our gracious hostess escorted us to a fabulous booth, overlooking the entire restaurant. It was *the* place to "see and be seen."

The risotto appetizer may be the best taste I have ever had in my mouth. Everything about the evening—from the service to the food— was nothing short of perfect. And the small chocolate treat with a candle and "Happy Birthday" in icing on the side of the plate was a perfect topping to the total experience.

And I got a surprise when the bill arrived. Certainly, it was larger than the check at Ted's in Crothersville, Indiana. However, we spent no more for our evening at Spago's in Beverly Hills than we would have if we were dining at a top restaurant in Indianapolis.

Our evening at Spago's was the Ultimate Customer Experience.

The birthday plate to our room? *Never made it.* When I mentioned this to the front desk again as we checked out—to be certain I wasn't billed for something I did not receive—they apologized, and a "customer relations manager" gave me her card and indicated they would send something to the room . . . the *next* time we stayed with them.

They totally missed the point. How many milestone birthdays does a husband get to provide for his wife? If they can't get it right this time—or even try to make it right during our stay—why would I ever entrust them with repeat business?

How has Wolfgang Puck remained on top in the extraordinarily competitive culinary world?

Deliver not only what you promise. Deliver *more* than you promise.

Treat everyone like a star—even a couple from Indiana who won't ever have their picture taken by the paparazzi, but who *will* tell their friends, and return to be customers again when they have the opportunity.

What a revolutionary idea: be so distinctive at what you do that your customers want to repeat their experience—and tell their friends, so they will do business with you too.

By the way: are you *that* good?

What Are You Doing to Question and Disrupt the Customary?

As mentioned earlier, if you keep doing what you've always done, you're going to receive *less* than you have in the past. Your competition is tougher, and the marketplace is changing.

So a critical question is, how are you questioning the traditional and disrupting the status quo?

Here's one example: sales professionals are customarily compensated by commission. If you want to be distinctive, ask why that is assumed to be the case and, perhaps an even more important question, ask whether a commission-based sales team inhibits distinction.

In a highly engaging and thought-provoking conversation with the owners of a leading car dealership, we discussed the disconnection between the way the salespersons of the dealership earned their commissions, and the desire of the dealership to create a high level of customer experience, in order to stimulate and ensure significant loyalty.

Here's the heart of the challenge: commission sales staff make their wages through the generation and completion of transactions.

This can naturally cause some of them to believe that all of the "customer experience stuff" they are being required to do *isn't essential to their measurable success* as a salesperson.

As soon as a "deal" is closed, it is to their financial advantage (or so they think) to hit the bricks and start chasing down another prospect. Explaining the features of the car, introducing the customer to the service manager, and the other little points that create a better experience are often viewed by salespeople as barriers to making more commission, because it keeps them away from contact with additional opportunities for transactions.

Some auto dealerships, and other businesses such as electronics sales, have moved away from the traditional commission model, with varying degrees of success.

The fundamental problems are: how do you keep a salesperson motivated to sell if her compensation isn't tied to production? And how do you motivate her to do what's necessary to provide a total experience to the customer if she believes the only meaningful part of her job is transactional?

Those are tough questions, and it's an incredibly fine line that any management team and industry must examine. While leaders tend to think in longer terms (and they should), sales professionals naturally have a much shorter time line in mind. It's easy for them to overlook both the vital importance of the customer experience in creating more sales over the long haul and the role that customer experience has in generating enhanced profitability for both the dealership and the individual.

Here are some ideas you may want to consider:

FIRST, CLEARLY PROVE TO SALES PROFESSIONALS THAT BETTER EXPERIENCES GENERATE MORE TRANSACTIONS.

It's counterintuitive, but a fact. If you create a higher level of experience, people spend more . . . and more often . . . with you. Not only do they desire to repeat their business, but you become referable as well.

SECOND, CREATE A COMPENSATION POOL FOR THOSE SALESPEOPLE WHO SCORE EXTRAORDINARILY HIGH IN CUSTOMER EVALUATIONS.

Give them bonuses for repeat and referral business. (It's obviously a maxim of business that it's less expensive to keep a current customer than to go out and find a new one.) The more of *that* type of sale your business achieves, the less your overhead to acquire a customer. Share the enhanced profit margin with your sales team, and you'll stimulate more of what you desire.

THIRD, DON'T TOLERATE SHODDY, HIGH-PRESSURE TREATMENT OF CUSTOMERS AND PROSPECTS.

It shouldn't have to be stated; however, some managers will allow a salesperson having a good month to slide a bit on client follow-up. This hurts in two ways. First, the prospects that salesperson converted to customers will look elsewhere for their next purchase. Second, the referrals generated by this approach will be nonexistent, forcing you to spend more to get prospects to your door. If you let this kind of sales-person get away with this behavior, you're not only displaying that it is acceptable within your organization, but you're eventually cutting your own throat, as well.

DEVELOP PEOPLE WITHIN YOUR ORGANIZATION WHO CAN HANDLE THE EXPERIENCE IF THE SALESPEOPLE AREN'T PROVIDING IT.

Let's face it, I don't want my doctor to have to worry about the accuracy of patient billing in his office. I want her to do what she does best. If a sales professional isn't on top of creating the experience via follow-up and ongoing contact, don't let the ball drop. Get someone on your team who can make it happen.

FINALLY, TAKE RESPONSIBILITY.

For all of our previous conversation about Circuit City in this book, we should also note the more recent development that electronics giant Best Buy is closing fifty of their big-box stores nationwide. This makes H. H. Gregg's overall story of success even more compelling, even if Gregg's encounters brief periods of challenge in the future. (To be fair, I also see Best Buy is opening 100 small, mobile locations at the same time.)

However, it's not the change, rather it is *how the change was explained* in Best Buy's case that caused a bit of amusement. According to an Associated Press story from March 29, 2012, Goldman Sachs analyst Matthew Fassler says, echoing the sentiments of the retailer, that, "Competitive pressure may be drifting into market share as well as margin, with Apple stores and Amazon.com the two most likely culprits."

It sounds similar to the time when Circuit City filed for bankruptcy in 2008, they said they were, "especially hard hit by the slowdown in consumer spending and the clampdown in the credit markets."

The United States Postal Service is losing billions of dollars. Their response is to close locations, raise prices, and become even more difficult to deal with.

My longtime friend and noted author and speaker Mark Sanborn of *The Fred Factor* fame related on Facebook his trials and tribulations with

United Airlines. Most discomforting was the fact that as a top-tier flier with more than 2 million miles on the airline under his belt, Mark still couldn't get anyone—not one person—with the company to assist him when he needed help.

So, just one time, wouldn't you love it if a CEO would call a press conference and say the following:

Ladies and gentlemen,

Our company has made a great error that we will begin to fix from this moment forward.

Certainly, we have some stores that haven't been profitable in the past few months. And let's face it, our competition is pretty darned good. In fact, they've been kicking our corporate butts for quite a while now.

I could stand up here and blame the economy . . . or a slowdown in consumer spending . . . or that we must be focused upon quarterly returns to protect our shareholders' investment in us . . . or any of those excuses you hear anytime a CEO like me tries to defend why his or her company is getting their lunch handed to them.

What all of that traditional talk wants you to forget is that someone else in our industry is doing pretty well. Apple and Amazon are growing. Southwest has been profitable. Other financial services firms didn't need bailouts and managed to keep their customers in the tent. If *they* didn't succumb to all of the economic, demographic, societal, global competitive, yada yada yada pressures, why did *we*?

We screwed up. We forgot customers want to be served.

Somehow, in focusing so much on EBITDA results and P&L statements, we just messed up on perhaps the single-most important aspect in economics: *If you ain't got customers, you ain't got a business.*

So, instead of closing locations and terminating employees, we are going to bust our tails to start giving customers a better experience than they can get anywhere else.

Sure, it's a risk. But what's the alternative? Death by a thousand cuts? Launch the slow death spiral most declining businesses take?

We can't shrink our way to distinction as a company. But we can and will *serve* our way there.

If you're our customer, you will receive an Ultimate Customer Experience. If you don't get it, I want to know about it. As the CEO, it will be my obsession. I will focus upon this to the practical exclusion of other priorities. This matters more than anything—and the very future of our company depends upon it.

We will become a joy to do business with—and it starts right here, right now, today.

Thank you very much.

I would love to hear one—just one—CEO have the intestinal fortitude and vision to try it.

However, the next time it happens will be the *first* time it has happened. And all we can do is wonder why.

Why are so many so unable to create distinction? In part, it's because there are additional aspects to it.

- We have to *deliver distinction* directly to our customers and bridge the gaps that disconnect us from them.
- We have to *extend distinction*, to ensure we don't merely gain the customer's business and fail to retain it.

- *We have to grow our distinction* to further establish our position of market leadership.
- And speaking of "leadership," it's easy to talk about it; however, actually *leading distinction* in our organization—becoming a leader of true distinction—is both incredibly important and remarkably difficult.

These facets will be explored in future books. For the time being, however, let's conclude our journey into the creation of distinction by learning what happened to the small-town grocery store.

TEN

DISTINCTIVE IS SUPERIOR

Long after Kern's Grill closed its doors in Crothersville, Indiana, Ted's Restaurant continued to thrive.

Its owner, Ted Zollman, was very clear about what his place of business was—and wasn't. Unlike Alvie Kern, Ted attempted to replicate neither the speed of McDonald's transactions nor the menu of Burger King. He got creative with his promotions and with his service. He communicated in a personal and charismatic manner with all who entered his establishment, and he created an Ultimate Customer Experience for just about everyone who dined there. After his passing, Ted's family sold the restaurant, and it remains in business to this day. Ted Zollman ran a small business, but, for me, he looms large among professionals skilled in providing Ultimate Customer Experiences.

I stand in awe of the accomplishments of Dr. Nido Qubein at High Point University. Although it has always been a wonderful institution, it has only recently begun to attain national attention and distinction. In my opinion, this is because of the remarkable job that Qubein has done to differentiate the school from its myriad of worthy competitors. A trip to the campus is one of the most invigorating and inspiring college visits anyone could have. You can almost feel the electricity in the air, and it is contagious.

As we have discussed, HPU has clarity about its purpose and has developed remarkably creative approaches to campus life and academics that are reverberating across the nation and—guided by its eloquent president—are being communicated to its varied audiences of students, parents, prospects, faculty, staff, and donors in an extraordinary manner.

And Nido Qubein clearly demonstrates his personal commitment to these principles. He teaches a class that is required for all freshmen: Real World 101: The President's Seminar on Life Skills. Not only does this class prepare HPU students for what life will bring them, both as college students and as graduates; it also means that every student will have spent time communicating with and getting to know the president of the university.

When you create compelling experiences for your clients, whether they are voters, students, guests at your diner, or grocery-store shoppers, they remember your product or service in a more frequent and significant manner.

My Best Teacher

Of all the businesspeople I have known, however, I learned the most about business and customers from my late father, Dallas McKain.

As I mentioned previously, my mom and dad owned the solitary grocery store in our rural community. After Dad worked for several years as a truck driver, meat cutter, then assistant grocery store manager, my parents finally rounded up the financing necessary to purchase a store of their own in our hometown. As is the case with many entrepreneurial couples, the future of our entire family depended upon the success of that little store, and my parents worked there tirelessly.

I remember Mom and Dad being somewhat shocked and highly concerned over the closing of Kern's Grill just across the street. For a family business to go under so quickly because of what my folks perceived to be issues totally out of their control caused enormous consternation. Then we received what was, for us, extremely tragic news: a new super-market was going to be built on the other end of our town.

It was going to have multiples of our modest shelf space. It would have a shiny linoleum floor, compared to our old wooden one. It would have more than one checkout lane, while we had a solitary, outdated NCR cash register. It would have what one good ol' boy back home called "the seeing-eye door." You would just walk up and it would *open*! (How could it *know*?) We certainly didn't have anything like that.

Many in our small town predicted that McKain's Market would be the next casualty to larger and supposedly more sophisticated competi-tion. However, Dad was just not ready to throw in the towel.

I reminisce now in what an old-timer back home calls "slack-jawed amazement" at some of my father's remarkable decisions.

He was armed with only a high school education and incredible instinct. He had no management training and had never previously owned a business, yet he made remarkable choices in the face of a sea change the size of "the perfect storm" for his little store.

He reduced the number of employees to only those who could and would remember every customer's name and make customers feel as if they were at home. He cut the number of hours our store was going to be open, instead of following the plan most small stores execute when a bigger box comes to town—staying open later to match their new competitor.

Dad's belief was that tired, stressed-out, worn-out employees do not create happy customers. Only about 5 percent of purchases were made during 20 percent of the time we were open, so, he reasoned, chop off some of those hours and rest your staff while reducing your overhead.

He emphasized the areas of service where he could differentiate our store from what he knew instinctively that the new competition would do.

He planted himself behind the counter and hand-cut and hand-wrapped almost every piece of meat the store sold. He designed a truck he could take to farms, so he could custom-butcher cattle. His thinking was that not only would the custom-butchering provide a significant new source of revenue for the store, but it would also be considerably more difficult for the farmer's family to then buy bread and milk at the competition when "good ol' Dallas" had literally been on their farm helping them.

> *Dad emphasized the areas of service that would differentiate our store from what the new competition would do.*

He also concentrated on what we were not (and could never become): a low-price leader. He knew that we would, by no means, be able to sell Green Giant creamed corn, for example, less expensively than a national competitor. Therefore, because we certainly could not be cheaper, we would have to be *different*.

I still clearly remember the day the competition opened. A nearby radio station did a live remote broadcast there—quite an event for our little town. It was Saturday, the busiest day in the grocery business, and as we drove by, we saw their parking lot was already jam-packed.

We entered McKain's Market practically in the shadow of the now-closed Kern's Grill and turned on the lights. It was seven a.m.

My sister, Shelley, made herself busy by pulling shelves. (That means you reach back into the shelves and pull the older cans to the front so that older stock sells before the newer product. If you just put the newest delivery at the front, the product in the back never changes.)

Mom shuffled papers in the tiny store office, and Dad was behind the meat counter grinding beef into hamburger for that day's sales. I took my spot behind our sole cash register, waiting to check out customers.

Imagine our feeling of depression and desperation when we had yet to serve our first customer *four hours* later! By that point, Mom was crying, and Dad was talking to himself. Shelley pulled every can in the store, and I plopped myself onto a stool to read the latest edition of *Superman*.

But as the clock was striking eleven, the door to our little store opened, and in walked the least likely customer imaginable. For the purposes of my story, let's call him Leland; he was what everyone in our town would call "quite a character." Suffice it to say, his reputation was less than sterling and his demeanor less than elegant.

Leland wrestled a shopping cart out of the stack and pulled out a slip of paper that, because of its neatness and precision, was obviously written by his wife. He started down the first aisle, muttering to himself and roughly throwing the items from his list into his cart.

As he continued to shop, my curiosity got the best of me, and by the time he arrived to be checked out, I was bursting to ask the question I had been pondering. I just could not keep it inside. It was a defining moment in my life—the point I realized I was endlessly fascinated with topics I later learned to describe as the behavior of customers and the differentiation of organizations.

"Leland," I began softly—after all, he was an adult and I was a mere schoolkid—"you, sir, are our first customer today."

He arched his right eyebrow and grunted.

"What I have to know is this, and I hope you don't mind me asking," I quickly added. "Why are you here? All of our so-called friends have left us today and gone to the supermarket owned by big shots from elsewhere. Why did you decide to come here instead of shop there?"

I will never forget what happened next.

Leland's face turned red as the tomatoes in his basket. He pawed his left boot awkwardly across our wooden floor. He glanced up at me and gruffly said, "Aw, come on. You know why."

I was at a loss. I just didn't get it. I had no idea why he had selected McKain's Market at that monumental moment. "No, Leland. I'm sorry. I don't know why."

Summoning up all of his communication ability, Leland looked me in the eye, a wry smile evolving from the right corner of his lips, and proudly announced, "Cause you guys *like me*!"

I'm a bit ashamed to admit that what popped into my head were words I would never utter: *No, we don't!*

Of course, my next thought was, *But we sure do now!*

Leland continued to shop with us, despite the advantages of our competition. Eventually, almost everyone else in town came back, too. Dad's little joke was that even if you only bought a pack of gum, we were going to carry it out to your car for you unless you wrestled us to the ground.

The marketplace in a small town in Indiana voted with their hard-earned grocery money and their feet. They decided that paying just a little more to shop where you received an Ultimate Customer Experience was a great investment.

> *Customers in a small Indiana town decided that paying a little more to shop where you had an Ultimate Customer Experience was a great investment.*

One time when I called home from college, I noticed Dad seemed a little bit down and not himself. When I asked why, he gave me the news: the supermarket had announced it was going to close and leave town.

"Good grief, Dad," I exclaimed, "you won! You beat the big store!"

"Aw, son," he replied, "what about those folks who work there? I just can't hire them all, and I don't want them to be out of work."

Of course, his sincere response was a perfect reflection of why people in Crothersville, Indiana, had considered the alternatives—and chosen to do business with *him*.

And that is how a simple meat cutter from a small Hoosier town inspired a business philosophy that his grateful son now has the privilege to write and teach to major corporations and visionary professionals around the world.

You Can Do It

The easiest tactic for you is to merely continue what you are currently doing. You may perceive that to "not make waves" and to "keep on keeping on" are the safest things for you to do. Let me emphatically state my belief that in the vast majority of cases, this is the most dangerous approach.

Because of the Three Destroyers of Differentiation, your job—from an organizational and an individual perspective—is only going to continue to increase in difficulty.

However, if you start today to chart a fresh approach based on the Four Cornerstones of Distinction, you can begin to enhance your organization while you nurture and grow yourself.

Create differentiation. Build distinction. It will make all the difference.

One More Thought . . .

After my father passed away, my sister and I were standing by the casket, awaiting the beginning of visitation hours to greet friends and family as they would pay their respects. Mark Adams, Crothersville's sole funeral home director, approached us with an amazed look on his face.

"I've never seen anything like it," he told us. "The waiting line is really long to see your dad." Shelley and I made some generic comment, then the funeral director added, "You don't get it. The line wraps around the funeral home, then goes for blocks down the street! I've never seen anything like it."

Many years after my family had sold our little grocery store, and a long time after Dad had moved away, our neighbors from a small country town still remembered the experience they received when they were his customers.

I can think of no better example. Develop a business and career of distinction. Create ultimate experiences for your customers, and they will never forget you.

RESOURCES

It is my hope and desire that you will continue to learn about strategic differentiation and what you can do to build distinction in the marketplace.

To that purpose, here is a list of resources—both in print and online—you may use to grow and share your knowledge.

You'll find a more complete collection on the website for this book: http://CreateDistinction.com.

Outstanding Business and Professional Development Books

The Eight Competencies of Relationship Selling: How to Reach the Top 1% in Just 15 Extra Minutes a Day by Jim Cathcart (Leading Authorities Press).

The Fred Factor by Mark Sanborn (Doubleday Business).

How to Be a Great Communicator: In Person, on Paper, and on the Podium by Nido Qubein (High Point University Press).

It's the Will, Not the Skill: Principles and Philosophies of Success by Jim Tunney (Success Publishing).

The Magic of Thinking Big by David Schwartz (Fireside).

Mastery: The Keys to Success and Long-Term Fulfillment by George Leonard (Plume).

My Father's Hand: A Daughter's Reflections on a Father's Wisdom by Naomi Rhode (Executive Books).

The One-Minute Entrepreneur: The Secret to Creating and Sustaining a Successful Business by Ken Blanchard, Don Hutson, and Ethan Willis (Doubleday Business).

The Platinum Rule: Discover the Four Basic Business Personalities and How They Can Lead You to Success by Tony Alessandra and Michael J. O'Connor (Grand Central Publishing).

Service America in the New Economy by Karl Albrecht and Ron Zemke (McGraw-Hill).

The SPEED of Trust: The One Thing That Changes Everything by Stephen M. R. Covey (Free Press).

The Tipping Point: How Little Things Can Make a Big Difference by Malcolm Gladwell (Back Bay Books).

Values-Based Financial Planning: The Art of Creating and Inspiring Financial Strategy by Bill Bachrach (Aim High Publishing).

The Voice of Authority: 10 Communication Strategies Every Leader Needs to Know by Dianna Booher (McGraw-Hill).

Blogs

Here are a select few of many wonderful blogs I've discovered that deal with differentiation and the customer experience. You'll find a more complete list at http://CreateDistinction.com.

All Business

http://www.allbusiness.com/sales/customerservice/10783-1.html

Ben Edwards's Marketing Blog

http://writemarketinggroup.blogspot.com/2005/03/
differentiation-is-key-to-real-success.html

Blog Toplist

http://www.blogtoplist.com/rss/customer-service.html

Brand Blog

http://brand.blogs.com/mantra/customer_experience/index.html

Branding Strategy

http://www.brandingstrategyinsider.com/2007/11/creating-brands.html

Client Service Blog

http://www.clientservice.blogspot.com/

Customer Experience Center

http://www.customerexperiencecenter.org/

Customer Experience Matrix

http://customerexperiencematrix.blogspot.com/

Customer Experience Matters

http://experiencematters.wordpress.com/

Customer Service

http://customerservice.blog.co.uk/

Customer Service King

http://www.customerserviceking.com/category/customer-service/

Differentiation Strategy

http://www.1000ventures.com/business_guide/be_different.html

Duct Tape Marketing Blog

http://ducttapemarketing.com/

Passion for the Good Customer Experience

http://p4tgce.blogspot.com/

Service Untitled

http://www.serviceuntitled.com

Seth Godin's Blog

http://sethgodin.typepad.com/

Shep Hyken

http://shephyken.blogspot.com/

Unique Marketing Ideas

http://www.unmarketing.com

NOTES

Introduction

1. Gary McWilliams, "Wal-Mart Era Wanes Amid Big Shifts in Retail," Wall Street Journal, October 3, 2007.
2. John A. Pearce and Richard B. Robinson, Strategic Management: Formulation, Implem*entation, and Control*, 8th ed. (New York: McGraw-Hill, 2003).

Chapter 1

1. Ron Waite, "Turbo Tennis," Tennis Server, August 2006, http://www.tennisserver.com.
2. Michael LeBoeuf, How to Win Customers and Keep Them for Life, rev. ed. (New York: Berkley Trade, 2000); GMP: The Greatest Management Principle in the World (New York: Putnam, 1985).
3. EricSchlosser, FastFoodNation (Boston: HoughtonMifflin, 2001), p. 233.
4. Scott McKain, What Customers REALLY Want (Nashville: Thomas Nelson, 2006).
5. Jim Rohn, The Art of Exceptional Living (Chicago: Nightingale-Conant).
6. "Montgomery Ward," http://en.wikipedia.org/wiki/ Montgomery_Ward.

Chapter 2

1. Ric Flair with Keith Elliot Greenberg, *Ric Flair: To Be the Man* (New York: Pocket Books, 2005).

2. Kurt Eichenwald, "Microsoft's Lost Decade," Vanity Fair, August 2012.

3. Ibid.

4. Matt Krantz, "Online Brokers Step Up Competition With Free Trades," USA Today, January 15, 2008.

5. Andrea Holecek, "The Dirt on Dry Cleaners," Munster Times [Indiana], January 18, 2004.

6. Joe Edwards, Nation's Restaurant News, June 4, 1984.

7. "Shoppers are Irriatated and Bored," The Grocer, October 22, 2005.

Chapter 3

1. "MacBooks 91% of Premium notebook market," Electronista.com; July 23, 2009.

2. Michael Porter, Competitive Advantage: Creating and Sustaining Superior Performance (New York: Free Press, 1985).

3. Mark Gillies, Automotive Magazine, 2002.

4. Chris Woodyard, "Mercedes-Benz A-Class aims for entry-level buyers," USA Today, March 6, 2012.

5. Ron Jonash, "Product Innovation: Staying Ahead of the Competition," USA Today Magazine, January 1, 2000.

6. Nick Churchouse, "Only One in Three Happy with Service," The Press (Christchurch, New Zealand), December 8, 2007.

7. EUCG, Inc., PR Newswire (Denver, Colorado), October 22, 2007.

Chapter 5

1. Janet Adamy, "Starbucks Closes Stores to Retrain Baristas," Wall Street Journal, February 27, 2008.

2. Amy Chulik, "Howard Shultz on How Starbucks Got Its Groove Back," The Hiring Site, June 3, 2011.

3. David Brody, CBN News broadcast, (http://www.cbn.com/CBNnews/475966.aspx) November 4, 2008.

Chapter 6

1. Alan G. Robinson and Sam Stern, Corporate Creativity (San Francisco: Berrett-Koehler, 1998).

2. Bruce D. Airo, Supervision, November 2006.

3. Ibid.

4. Stefi Weisburd, Science News, November 1987.

5. Bryan Ochalla, Credit Union Management, August 2003.

6. R&D, October 1988.

7. Jonah Lehrer, "Groupthink," The New Yorker, January 30, 2012.

8. Ken Blanchard and Barbara Glanz, The Simple Truths of Service: Inspired by Johnny the Bagger (Blanchard Family Partnership, 2005).

9. William M. Luther, The Marketing Plan: How to Prepare and Implement It, 3rd ed. (New York: AMACOM, 2001), p. 120.

10. Andrei Codrescu, commentary aired on All Things Considered, September 21, 2001.

11. "Build Your Business Through Non-traditional Sales & Marketing Techniques," Motor, May 2005.

12. "Obama 2.0 Marketing," http://obama20marketing.blogspot.com.

13. Wagner James Au, "Confirmed: Obama Is Campaigning on Xbox 360!, http://gigaom.com/2008/10/13/confirmed-obama is-campaigning-on-xbox-360/ (accessed on November 4, 2009).

14. Dr. Jac Fitz-enz, "The Truth About 'Best Practice,' " Human Resource Planning, September 1993.

15. Ibid.

16. Jim Collins, Good to Great (New York: Collins, 2001).

17. Forbes.com, February 26, 2008.

18. Michael Felberbaum, "Circuit City Closing 155 Stores," Associated Press, November 3, 2008.

19. Don Reisinger, C-net News, http://news.cnet.com/circuit-city execs-killed-the-company/ (accessed on November 4, 2009).

20. Sandra M. Jones, "Walgreens Open to Change," *Chicago Tribune*, October 31, 2008.

21. "Guru Peters Still Taking No Prisoners," http://www.theage.com.au/ articles/2003/11/20/1069027253087.html (accessed July 8, 2012).

22. Collins, *Good to Great.*

23. David S. Hilzenrath, "Report Slams Fannie Mae: U.S. Regulators Find Accounting Failures at Housing Financier," *Washington Post,* September 23, 2004.

24. Lisa BaerHein and Nicholas Groom, "Starbucks Splashes Outlook, Blames Housing Meltdown," Reuters, April 23, 2008.

25. Andrea James, "Starbucks Profit Takes Bitter Shot for the Year," *Seattle Post-Intelligencer,* November 11, 2008.

Chapter 7

1. Hilary McLellan of McLellan Wyatt Digital, http://www. tech-head.com.

2. Excerpted from "Obama: Victory Speech," *New York Times*, November 5, 2008 (Accessed November 6, 2009).

3. Joseph Campbell, The Hero with a Thousand Faces, 2nd ed. (Novato, Calif.: New World Library, 2008); George Lucas statement appears in A Fire in the Mind: The Life of Joseph Campbell by Stephen and Robin Larsen (New York: Doubleday, 1991).

4. Ibid.

5. Mary E. Boyce, "Organizational Story and Storytelling: A Critical Review," Journal of Organizational Change (1996).

6. Peter Burrows, "The Mac in the Gray Flannel Suit," *Business Week,* May 12, 2008.

7. CNN report, September 28, 1998, http://www.cnn.com/SHOWBIZ/ Movies/9809/28/screen.test/ (accessed July 8, 2012).

8. Ibid.

Chapter 8

1. Customers Are Always; http://www.customersarealways.com (accessed November 13, 2009).

2. Maria Palma, "What Is a Customer-Focused Strategy?" Customers Are Always, May 10, 2008, http://www. customersarealways.com/2008/05/what_is_a_customerfocused_stra.html (accessed November 13, 2009).

3. "Shared Belief in the 'Golden Rule,' or The Ethics of Reciprocity," ReligiousTolerance.org (the Web site of Ontario Consultants on Religious Tolerance), http://www. religioustolerance.org/aboutus.htm (accessed November 15, 2009).

Chapter 9

1. Brent Schlender, "The Lost Steve Jobs Tapes," *Fast Company*, April 18, 2012.

ACKNOWLEDGMENTS

Every single day, I am grateful for the work of Shelley Erwin. She serves McKain Performance Group as the vice president of marketing but is, in fact, our chief operating officer, handling all of the day-to-day work, so I can write books and present speeches. (She's also my favorite—and *only*—sister!) Perry Cremeans is our director of content services and creates UCEs for our clients, enabling us to show the world we "walk our talk."

For many years, Clint Greenleaf and I have talked about doing a book together, and I am thrilled our mutual dream has turned into reality. The entire team at Greenleaf—especially Justin Branch getting the deal done, Chris McRay shepherding the project, Ben Dunlop for distribution, Brian Phillips for his brilliant design, and more—have been magnificent. It's the beginning of a wonderful ride together.

No one could have better professional colleagues than I possess with my fellow members of Speakers Roundtable. Their generosity is amazing and their friendship beyond description. It is such an honor to be a part of this group. Thanks, as well, to the speakers bureaus and my many clients across the country and around the world that keep my calendar full.

Scott Stratten, author of the brilliant *UnMarketing*, has been a mind-blowing source of inspiration and ideas.

Heartfelt appreciation to the best friends a guy could have—my pals in the greatest band in the history of country music (okay, I'm biased),

Diamond Rio. Thanks to my best buddies, Brian Prout and Dana Williams, along with Gene Johnson, Jimmy Olander, Dan Truman, and Marty Roe. (And road manager Danny Beard!) You guys rock! (But not too much—you're a *country* band!)

I'm also appreciative of the support and my renewed friendship (after several decades) with the legendary Oak Ridge Boys. William Lee Golden has been a real mentor with his vision and integrity. It's hard to describe how much it means to me that he truly cares about our friendship! Richard Sterban is a model of hard work and dynamic manners. Duane Allen is the guy I always wanted to be when I was a teen—smooth, sophisticated, and polished. It's great to know that some things never change. Finally, there's not a better guy on the planet than Joe Bonsall. His books are inspirational, his stories compelling, and his talent limitless. He's a true friend. Thanks, too, to Darrick Kinslow—a great buddy who keeps the wheels going for one of the greatest acts in music history.

In addition, a chance meeting as we sat side by side on a Delta flight from Atlanta to Las Vegas introduced me to one of the most distinctive thinkers I've ever encountered: Zac Brown of the Zac Brown Band. I'll be writing more about him in a future book; meanwhile, I'm grateful for the insights he has shared in our brief acquaintance.

Thom Chitton edited the original manuscript with a commitment that was quite impressive. Heather Skelton took the ball and carried the project across the finish line. And Patricia Fogarty has done a remarkable job in getting the book revised, re-edited, and relaunched. I am grateful to all three for making *Create Distinction* all that it could be, especially given the material at your disposal. My sincere thanks to Jason Jones for his initial work leading the effort to tell the world about this book. James Levesque and Shellie Wilkinson and Levesque-Wilkinson Media

Relations are greatly appreciated for their efforts to keep my ideas and work in front of the press.

Kudos, too, to Ted Greene at Modern Management for his years of partnership and Mel Berger at William Morris Agency for giving me a first chance at being an author.

Saving the best for last, I'm most grateful to a wonderful woman who was willing to take a chance on this lost soul and worried widower at a time that I wasn't at my best. My bride, Tammy, somehow believed in me to the point that she moved from her hometown and allowed me to share the life that she had built with her two wonderful sons. Even though I make my living with words, I find myself ill-equipped to describe how grateful I am that you are my partner and in my life . . . every day. I love you.

And to all of *you* . . . thank you for reading. My sincere desire is that your time and effort has been well spent with *Create Distinction*.

Scott McKain

ABOUT THE AUTHOR

Scott McKain is chairman of McKain Performance Group, Inc., a highly successful company specializing in educating visionary organizations and professionals on business growth through strategic differentiation. He is also cofounder and principal of the Value Added Institute, a think tank that focuses on the growth of client retention and acquisition through enhanced customer experiences.

Scott McKain's calling is business, but his passion is the platform. He presents compelling programs on creating distinction in the marketplace through the development of an Ultimate Customer Experience for visionary organizations that seek to expand their impact and profitability. He has presented programs for the world's leading organizations at meetings and conferences—before audiences as large as 20,000 in all fifty states and more than fifteen nations, from Morocco to Malaysia, from Singapore to Sweden.

He is a member of the Professional Speakers Hall of Fame and of Speakers Roundtable, a historic and elite association of twenty professional speakers and consultants recognized as the market leaders in their respective fields.

From thousands of nominees, he was recognized in his home state as one of ten "Hoosier Heroes" for his commitment to charitable involvement and philanthropy.

To Contact Scott McKain

To get in touch with Scott McKain regarding his keynote presentations, training seminars, online learning modules, or any of the many other ways he can be of service to your organization to help create distinction and grow your business, contact:

Shelley Erwin
Vice President of Marketing
McKain Performance Group, Inc.
11650 Olio Road
Suite #1000-323
Fishers, IN 46037
1-800-838-6980

contact@ScottMcKain.com

Keep in touch online with everything Scott McKain:
http://ScottMcKain.com
http://McKainViewpoint.com (Scott's blog)
http://ProjectDistinct.com (a daily thought on creating distinction)
http://UltimateCustomerExperience.com
http://CreateDistinction.com